First World War
and Army of Occupation
War Diary
France, Belgium and Germany

58 DIVISION
Divisional Troops
511 Field Company Royal Engineers
26 January 1917 - 31 May 1919

WO95/2996/6

The Naval & Military Press Ltd
www.nmarchive.com
Published in association with The National Archives

Published by

The Naval & Military Press Ltd

Unit 10 Ridgewood Industrial Park,

Uckfield, East Sussex,

TN22 5QE England

Tel: +44 (0) 1825 749494

www.naval-military-press.com

www.nmarchive.com

This diary has been reprinted in facsimile from the original. Any imperfections are inevitably reproduced and the quality may fall short of modern type and cartographic standards.

© **Crown Copyright**
Images reproduced by permission of The National Archives, London, England, 2015.

Contents

Document type	Place/Title	Date From	Date To
Heading	WO95/2996/6		
Heading	War Diary 511 Field Coy R.E Vol 192		
War Diary	Le Havre	26/01/1917	28/01/1917
War Diary	Auxi-Le-Chateau	29/01/1917	29/01/1917
War Diary	Villers L' Hopital	01/02/1917	01/02/1917
War Diary	Henu	01/02/1917	01/02/1917
War Diary	Villers L' Hopital	05/02/1917	05/02/1917
War Diary	Grenas	15/02/1917	21/02/1917
War Diary	Bailleulmont	24/02/1917	25/02/1917
Heading	War Diary Of 511 Field Co RE From 27/2/17 To 15/3/17 Vol 3		
War Diary	Bailleulmont	27/02/1917	03/03/1917
War Diary	La Bazeque	03/03/1917	03/03/1917
War Diary	Bailleulmont	03/03/1917	12/03/1917
War Diary	La Cauchie	12/03/1917	12/03/1917
War Diary	Bailleulmont	13/03/1917	15/03/1917
Heading	War Diary Of 511 Field Coy R.E. From 26/3/17 To 31/3/17 Volume II		
War Diary	Berles-Au-Bois	26/03/1917	26/03/1917
War Diary	Adinfer	26/03/1917	26/03/1917
War Diary	Lucheux	27/03/1917	31/03/1917
Heading	War Diary Of 511 Field Co. R.E. From 16/3/17 To 24/3/17 Volume II		
War Diary	Bailleulmont	27/02/1917	03/03/1917
War Diary	La Bazeque	03/03/1917	03/03/1917
War Diary	Bailleulmont	03/03/1917	12/03/1917
War Diary	La Cauchie	12/03/1917	12/03/1917
War Diary	Bailleulmont	13/03/1917	25/03/1917
Heading	War Diary Of 511 Field Coy R.E. From 1/4/17 To 25/4/17 Volume II		
War Diary	Lucheux	01/04/1917	01/04/1917
War Diary	Ligny-Sur-Canche	02/04/1917	02/04/1917
War Diary	Lucheux	02/04/1917	02/04/1917
War Diary	Cheriennes	03/04/1917	04/04/1917
War Diary	Bourquemaison	05/04/1917	05/04/1917
War Diary	Hem	05/04/1917	05/04/1917
War Diary	Auchonvillers	06/04/1917	06/04/1917
War Diary	Mailly-Maillet	07/04/1917	07/04/1917
War Diary	Bihucourt	08/04/1917	25/04/1917
War Diary	Reference Map 57c-NW	26/04/1917	30/04/1917
War Diary	Map Ref:- 51c-N.W.	01/05/1917	05/05/1917
War Diary	Reference Map 57c N.W.	06/05/1917	26/05/1917
War Diary	Bullecourt	26/05/1917	31/05/1917
War Diary	Map Ref 57c-N.W.	01/06/1917	03/06/1917
War Diary	Bullecourt	04/06/1917	05/06/1917
War Diary	Map Ref 57c-N.W.	06/06/1917	15/06/1917
War Diary	Bullecourt	16/06/1917	16/06/1917
War Diary	Bullecourt Map Ref. 57c-N.W.	16/06/1917	18/06/1917
War Diary	Map Ref 57C NW	18/06/1917	29/07/1917
War Diary	Fosseux	30/07/1917	31/07/1917

War Diary	Map Ref. 51c P.16.a.6.8 Fosseux	01/08/1917	10/08/1917
War Diary	Map Ref. 57c P16a.0.2 Fosseux	11/08/1917	19/08/1917
War Diary	Duisans	20/08/1917	24/08/1917
War Diary	Ypres Area	25/08/1917	27/08/1917
War Diary	Map Ref. 28. Ypres Area	27/08/1917	31/08/1917
War Diary	Map Reference 28 Sheet Ypres Salient	01/09/1917	27/09/1917
War Diary	Hazebrouck 5E	28/09/1917	28/09/1917
War Diary	Calais 13	28/09/1917	30/09/1917
War Diary	Map Ref:- Calais 13. F.3. Sanghen	01/10/1917	08/10/1917
War Diary	Sanghen	09/10/1917	09/10/1917
War Diary	Map. 28.N.W.	10/10/1917	31/10/1917
War Diary	Map 28 N.W. Ypres Salient	01/11/1917	06/11/1917
War Diary	Map 28 N.W.	07/11/1917	15/11/1917
War Diary	Map Ref. 19.SE. Proven Area	16/11/1917	19/11/1917
War Diary	Map 28 N.W. Ypres Area	19/11/1917	22/11/1917
War Diary	Map 28 N.W.	23/11/1917	27/11/1917
War Diary	Map Hazebrouck 5A	28/11/1917	28/11/1917
War Diary	Calais Map 13	28/11/1917	30/11/1917
War Diary	Calais Map 13	01/12/1917	01/12/1917
War Diary	Bainghem-Le-Comze	01/12/1917	05/12/1917
War Diary	Lumbres	06/12/1917	08/12/1917
War Diary	Map 28.N.W.	09/12/1917	22/12/1917
War Diary	Map 28 (Belgium)	22/12/1917	31/12/1917
Heading	511th (London) Field Co R.E. War Diary 1st-31st January 1918 Vol 13		
War Diary	Map 28. N.W.	01/01/1918	08/01/1918
War Diary	Map. 27.	08/01/1918	18/01/1918
War Diary	Map 27 Map Amiens	19/01/1918	25/01/1918
War Diary	Map Amiens	26/01/1918	26/01/1918
War Diary	Map St Quentin	27/01/1918	29/01/1918
War Diary	Map Sheet 66c S.W. Edition 2.A.	30/01/1918	24/02/1918
War Diary	Map. 10.D.N. W.	25/02/1918	28/02/1918
War Diary	Map. 10d. N.W. 1/20,000	01/03/1918	23/03/1918
War Diary	Sheets 10d. N.W. & 10 E	23/03/1918	31/03/1918
Heading	58th Div. War Diary 511th Field Company, R.E. April 1918		
War Diary	Maps 70 E. St. Quentin	01/04/1918	04/04/1918
War Diary	Map 62.D	05/04/1918	26/04/1918
War Diary	Map Lens (II) 1/100,000	27/04/1918	30/04/1918
Heading	War Diary Of 511th Field Coy. R.E. From 1-5-18 To 31-5-18 Vol 16		
War Diary	Coulonvillers Map Lens. II.	01/05/1918	05/05/1918
War Diary	Maps-Amiens	06/05/1918	10/05/1918
War Diary	57 D	06/05/1918	10/05/1918
War Diary	Map 57D	11/05/1918	14/05/1918
War Diary	Map 62D. N.W.	15/05/1918	27/05/1918
War Diary	Maps 62D. & 57d.	27/05/1918	31/05/1918
Heading	War Diary Of 511th (London) Field Coy R.E. For Period 1-6-18 To 30-6-18 Vol. XVII		
War Diary	France Map 62D	01/06/1918	04/06/1918
War Diary	Sheet 57d	05/06/1918	09/06/1918
War Diary	Map Amiens	10/06/1918	16/06/1918
War Diary	Map 62d.	17/06/1918	30/06/1918
War Diary	War Diary Of 511th (London) Field Co. R.E. For Period 1-7-18 To 31-7-18 Vol. XVIII		
War Diary	Maps 62dt Senlis	01/07/1918	31/07/1918

Heading	58th Divl. Engineers. 511th Field Company Royal Engineers August 1918		
War Diary	Map 62D	01/08/1918	03/08/1918
War Diary	Map. 62d. N.W.	04/08/1918	28/08/1918
War Diary	Map. 62 d. N.E.	29/08/1918	29/08/1918
War Diary	Map. 62c. N.W.	30/08/1918	31/08/1918
Heading	War Diary Of 511th (London) Field Coy R.E. (T) For Period 1-9-18 To 30-9-18 Vol.21		
War Diary	Map Sheet 62 C N.W.	01/09/1918	07/09/1918
War Diary	Map 62c. N.E.	08/09/1918	24/09/1918
War Diary	Map 62D.N.W.	24/09/1918	25/09/1918
War Diary	Map. Lens. 11.	26/09/1918	30/09/1918
Heading	War Diary Of 511th Field Coy R.E. For Period 1-10-18 To 31-10-18		
War Diary	Map Sheet 44 A	01/10/1918	31/10/1918
Heading	War Diary Of 511th Field Company R.E. For The Period 1.11.18 To 30.11.18.		
War Diary	Map Ref. Sheet 44	01/11/1918	09/11/1918
War Diary	Sheet 38	10/11/1918	28/11/1918
War Diary	Sheet 44	29/11/1918	30/11/1918
War Diary	Sheet 44 K.4.b.4.8. Wiers	01/12/1918	22/12/1918
War Diary	Sheet 44	23/12/1918	31/12/1918
War Diary	Wiers. Sheet 44. K.4.b.4.8	01/01/1919	31/01/1919
War Diary	Wiers, Belgium	01/02/1919	22/02/1919
War Diary	Leuze Belgium	22/02/1919	28/02/1919
War Diary	Leuze Belgium	01/03/1919	31/05/1919

WO 95/2996/6

58
Vol/42

WAR DIARY

511 FIELD Coy. R.E.

Army Form C. 2118.

WAR DIARY
INTELLIGENCE SUMMARY.
(Erase heading not required.)

Instructions regarding War Diaries and Intelligence Summaries are contained in F. S. Regs, Part II. and the Staff Manual respectively. Title pages will be prepared in manuscript.

Place	Date	Hour	Summary of Events and Information	Remarks and references to Appendices
LE HAVRE	26/1/17	5. P.M.	Disembarkation of Company completed. Company proceeded to HALLE 3, arriving 5.30 P.M.; marched to REST CAMP B, arriving at 7.45 p.m.	
LE HAVRE	27/1/17	4.30 p.m.	Left REST CAMP B. and marched to POINT I. for entrainment; train departed at 9.25 p.m.	
	28/1/17		Still en route.	
AUXI-LE-CHATEAU	29/1/17	13.20 p.m.	Detrained. Marched away at 2.15 a.m.; arrived at VILLERS L'HÔPITAL 4.40 a.m.; then billeted in barns, etc.; horses picketed out.	
VILLERS L'HÔPITAL	1/2/17	11.15 a.m.	5 Officers, 150 Other Ranks, 1 A.S.C. Driver (attached), 2 H.D. horses (attached) and dubbly Wagon proceeded to join 46th Divisional R.E. for 16 days' instruction.	
HENU.	1/2/17	2.15 p.m.	Above party arrived.	
VILLERS L'HÔPITAL	5/2/17	9.30 a.m.	Mounted Portion of Company proceeded from VILLERS L'HÔPITAL to GRENAS by road.	
GRENAS.	15/2/17		Dismounted Portion of Company came back from Trenches and re-assembled at GRENAS same day.	
GRENAS.	15/2/17		1 Officer and 50 other Ranks from each of 2/5th, 1/6th, 2/7th and 2/8th BATTALIONS, CITY OF LONDON REGIMENT, attached as BRIGADE PIONEER COMPANY. These men were billeted at HALLOY. LIEUT. E.A. SMITH left Unit.	
GRENAS.	16-2-17		Resting at GRENAS.	
GRENAS.	17-2-17		Resting at GRENAS.	

Army Form C. 2118.

WAR DIARY

~~INTELLIGENCE SUMMARY~~

(Erase heading not required.)

Instructions regarding War Diaries and Intelligence Summaries are contained in F. S. Regs., Part II. and the Staff Manual respectively. Title pages will be prepared in manuscript.

Place	Date	Hour	Summary of Events and Information	Remarks and references to Appendices
GRENAS.	18-2-17		Resting at GRENAS.	
GRENAS.	19-2-17		Advance Party, consisting of 2 Officers and 11 Other Ranks proceeded to BAILLEULMONT.	
GRENAS.	21-2-17	10.30am	Company and Pioneers attached proceeded from GRENAS to BAILLEULMONT to take over duties on Trenches lately held by 146th BRIGADE. R.E.	
BAILLEULMONT	24-2-17		Took over R.E. work on Trenches between BOUNDARY POST. W.18.a.0.2. and ENGINEER STREET. R.33.a.10.5, inclusive. (Reference Maps 51c. S.E. and 51b. S.W).	
	22-2-17 to 24-2-17		Working in trenches on revetting and improvement of C.Ts, mined dugouts, and strong points.	
BAILLEULMONT	25/2/17	2.10am	Orders received to be prepared to move at one hour's notice. Company stood to from 5.0. A.M. until 10.15 A.M. when orders were ~~received~~ cancelled.	

J. J. Bertram
Major R.E.
O/c 511 Field Co

To Complete 58
Vol 3

Confidential

War Diary
of
511 Field Co. RE

From 27/2/17 to 15/3/17

WAR DIARY
or
INTELLIGENCE SUMMARY.

Army Form C. 2118.

511th Field Coy. R.E.

Place	Date	Hour	Summary of Events and Information	Remarks and references to Appendices
BAILLEUMONT	27/2/17		Work on Strong Points, meeting, preparation of fire bays, machine gun emplacements, dug-outs &c.	
			Meeting near C.T.3 to branch system adjusted to this unit	
			O.C. saw Brigadier 174th Inf. Bde, and obtained from him permission to demolish LE GASTINEAU, and	F.9.15
			inspection was made for its demolition.	
			Pioneer Officer of 2/5th C.L. Regt admitted hospital (sick)	
			C.E. XVIII Corps inspected Workshops, BAVINCOURT	
			O.C. 511st Field Co. R.E. visited HANDOFF and LANARK WORKS with C.R.E. 58th Division and	
			obtained his approval of sites for rear fire trenches	
	28/2/17		Work on trench system as before. Preparation for demolition of LE GASTINEAU	F.9.15
			Twenty O.R., 37 animals & 6 G.S. wagons of D.A.C. 46th Division reported for transport duty for R.E. stores	
			O.C. 511st Field Co R.E. met second in command of 2/5th Home Counties Field Ambulance at O.36.c.8.8. with	F.9.15
			reference to erection of Advanced Dressing Station there, and the ladder promised to furnish dimensions	
			of dugout required. Works on trench system as before.	
	2/3/17		Demolition of LE GASTINEAU	F.9.15
			Message received from C.R.E. 58th Division (I.4/5 of 2nd inst) that the men, wagons attached to this unit	
			from D.A.C. 46th Division should be returned and that they would be replaced by wagons from D.A.C. 58th Division	

WAR DIARY or INTELLIGENCE SUMMARY.

Army Form C. 2118.

511th Field Coy. R.E.

(2)

Place	Date	Hour	Summary of Events and Information	Remarks and references to Appendices
BAILLEULMONT	2/5/17		1 Officer & 32 O.Rs. 7 animals & 1 Limbered G.S. wagon of 2nd Field Light R.E. reported for accommodation and rations to be under orders of C.R.E. 58th Division. Letter O.93 of 27/2/17	App. 18
	3/3/17		O.C. 511th Field Coy. R.E. met O.C. 195th M.G. Co. and agreed on sites of M.G. Es. in BOUNDARY POST.	
			LLANDAFF and LANARK LOOKS. Works on French system as before	
LA BAZEQUE	"		Received instructions from C.R.E. to procure water supply at La Bazeque Farm.	App. 18
			This was inspected and reported on. The work was being done by 141st Co. R.E. (info. verbal)	
			16 other ranks, 31 animals & 5 G.S. wagons reported for transport duty from D.A.C. 58th Division	
BAILLEULMONT	4/3/17		Work on French system as before.	
			3 Other Ranks, 6 animals & 1 G.S. wagon reformed from D.A.C. 58th Div. for transport work	App. 19
			Heavy hostile artillery shelling of front lines & C.T.s	
			Received message from HQ 174th Inf. Bde. (R.22 of 4/3/17) that trench line with sentries and by HQ was much damaged by shell fire and asking for assistance in carrying out repair. This was arranged	
			O.C. 511th Field Coy. R.E. visited with C.R.E. & set out O.Bs. for a garrison of 1 Platoon of Infantry on E. & W. sides of BELLACOURT and BRISEUX ROAD	
	10.30 am		Casualties 2/6th Bn. C.L. Regt. Dis-area attack A+ killed 2 OR Wounded + O.R. in LIVERICK LANE	

Army Form C. 2118.

(3)

511th Field Coy R.E

WAR DIARY
or
INTELLIGENCE SUMMARY.
(Erase heading not required.)

Instructions regarding War Diaries and Intelligence Summaries are contained in F. S. Regs., Part II. and the Staff Manual respectively. Title pages will be prepared in manuscript.

Place	Date	Hour	Summary of Events and Information	Remarks and references to Appendices
BAILLEULMONT	5/3/17		Work on trench system as before	
	6/3/17		R.E Camp at BAILLEULMONT shelled by the enemy with 4.2" and 5.9" H.E. and shrapnel shells. O.C. 511th Field Coy R.E arranged for repair of damage by shell fire to trenches and Coy H.Q's. Dugout at the forward end of LINCOLN LANE line in front of trenches repaired. Change of Front. (1) Handed over R.E supervision of trenches from BOUNDARY POST, inclusive, to ENGINEER ST and DYKE STREET, exclusive, with maps, plans &c relating to the work, and R.E dump, GROSVILLE, to 503rd Field Co R.E. (2) Took over R.E supervision of trench system from 21st STREET, inclusive, to W.28.d.85.38 in addition to present area (Ref. Map 51c S.E + 51 S.W.), O.C. 51st Field Co. R.E went to LA CAUCHIE to discuss with O.Cs. 21st + 2nd Field Australians works required at their camps. Latrine screens on BAILLEULMONT - LA CAUCHIE ROAD was inspected and arrangements made for re-erection. R.E. Camp at BAILLEULMONT shelled	2/9/18 7/9/18
	7/3/17		One Sapper Carpenter sent to supervise hut erection at LA CAUCHIE for 21st HC Field Ambulance. Work on trench system as before. No. 3 of Sections + attached Pioneers moved from BAILLEULMONT to BERLES. Half of No.3 Section & attached Pioneers moved from BAILLEULMONT to BELLACOURT.	9/9/18

Army Form C. 2118.

WAR DIARY
or
INTELLIGENCE SUMMARY.
(Erase heading not required.)

511th Field Coy R.E.

Instructions regarding War Diaries and Intelligence Summaries are contained in F. S. Regs., Part II. and the Staff Manual respectively. Title pages will be prepared in manuscript.

Place	Date	Hour	Summary of Events and Information	Remarks and references to Appendices
BAILLEULMONT	8/3/17		Work on trench system as before; heaving shelling, damage to front line and wire	919
	9/3/17		Making dugouts at BAILLEULMONT. Establishments:- 2 other ranks of D.A.C. 58th Division reported for duty.	
	9/3/17		1 L.D. horse sent to hospital with mange	919
	10/3/17 to 12/3/17		Work on trench system, as before; repairing wire Preparing dugouts at BAILLEULMONT Commander XVIII Corps inspected line from PARK STREET to RENFREW ROAD.	919
LA CAUCHIE			Improving Broomes Loage, BAILLEULMONT Particulars taken of platforms etc required by A.S.C. 174th Bde. Nine other ranks, 18 animals and 3 G.S. wagons of D.A.C. 58th Division detw red to unit.	919
BAILLEULMONT	13/3/17 to 15/3/17		Work on trench system, as before. Improving Prisoners Raye, BAILLEULMONT. Establishment:- 7 other ranks, 7 animals and 1 G.S. wagon of D.A.C. 58th Division returned to their unit. Work for improvement of water supply at BAILLEULMONT inspected. Improving Prisoners Loage. G.O.C. Third Army, G.O.C. 58th Division and B.O.G. 174th Inf. Bde. inspected right of trench system of the left sector. C.R.E. visited left sector. Work on trench system as before.	919

Vol #

War Diary
of
511 Field Coy. R.E.
From 26/3/17 to 31/3/17

Volume II

WAR DIARY

Army Form C. 2118.

511 FIELD COY R.E.

Place	Date	Hour	Summary of Events and Information	Remarks and references to Appendices
BEALES-AU-BOIS	26/3/17	9.30 a.m.	Coy H.Q., Nos. 2 & 4 Sections, 75th & 77th Pioneers attached, moved from BEALES-AU-BOIS to LUCHEUX.	A.1.8
ADINFER	"		Sections 1 and 3 with 76th and 78th Pioneers attached moved from ADINFER to LUCHEUX.	
LUCHEUX	27/3/17		All ranks of D.A.C., 582nd Division, attached to this Company, with horses and wagons, returned to Unit. Arms and equipment of Company and Pioneers attached inspected.	A.1.8
"	28/3/17		Infantry drill. Engineer reconnaissance of LUCHEUX District. Engineer training &c.	A.9.8
"	29/3/17		" and Engineer training.	A.9.8
"	30/3/17		Engineer training and route march.	A.9.8
"	31/3/17		Infantry drill. Engineer training. Orders received from C.R.E., 58th Division to move to LIGNY-SUR-CANCHE	A.9.8

J.J. Brewett
Major R.E.(T)
Commdg. 511 Field Coy R.E.

Vol 3

<u>Confidential</u>

War Diary
of
511 Field Co. R.E.

From   16/3/17   to   24/3/17

Volume <u>II</u>

Army Form C. 2118.

WAR DIARY
INTELLIGENCE SUMMARY.
(Erase heading not required.)

511 Field Coy RE

Place	Date	Hour	Summary of Events and Information	Remarks and references to Appendices
BAILLEUMONT	27/2/17		Work on Strong Points, revetting, preparation of fire bays, machine gun emplacements, dug-outs, &c. revetting main B.J.s in trench system allotted to this Unit.	AA18
			WO saw Brigadier, 174th Inf Bde and obtained from him permission to demolish LE CAUCHY NETTU and inspection was made for its demolition.	
			Pioneer Officer of 7th C.L. Regt admitted Hospital (sick).	
			C.E. XVIII Corps inspected Workshops, BAVINCOURT	
			WO, SM Field & RE visited LLANDAFF and LANARK WORKS with CRE 58th Division and named two approval of sites for new fire trenches	
	28/2/17		Work on French system as before. Preparation for demolition of LE CAUCHY NETTU.	AA19
			Twenty O.R., 3 animals & 6 G.S. wagons of DAC 46th Division reported for transport duty for RE Stores.	
	1/3/17		WO, 511 F.C. RE met Second in command of 7/3rd Home Counties Field Ambulance at Q 36.c 8.8 with reference to erection of Advanced Dressing Station there & the latter promised to furnish dimensions of dugout required. Work on French system as before.	AA20
	2/3/17		Demolition of LE CAUCHY NETTU. Works on trench system as before. Message received from CRE 58th Division (7:45 p.m. 2nd inst) that the men & wagons attached to this Unit from DAC 46th Division should be returned & that they would be replaced by wagons from DAC 58th Division.	AA21

Army Form C. 2118.

WAR DIARY
or
INTELLIGENCE SUMMARY.
(Erase heading not required.)

511 Field Coy R.E. (2)

Place	Date	Hour	Summary of Events and Information	Remarks and references to Appendices
BRILLEULMONT	7/3/17		1 Officer, 32 O.R., 7 animals + 1 limbered G.S. wagon of 2nd Field Sqdn R.E. reported for accommodation and rations (to be under orders of C.E. XVIII Corps. See C.R.E. 58th Division letter O.93 of 27/2/17)	A.A.1.
	3/3/17		O.C. 511 Field Coy R.E. met O.C. 178th M.G.C. and agreed on sites of M.G.E's in BOUNDARY POST, LLANDAFF and LANARK works. Works on trench system as before.	A.A.2.
LA BAZEQUE FARM	"		Received instructions from C.R.E. to examine water supply at LA BAZEQUE FARM. This was inspected + reported on. The work was being done by 1/1st C.E. R.E. (Corps Troops)	
BRILLEULMONT	"		16 other ranks, 21 animals + 5 G.S. wagons reported for transport duty from D.A.C. 58th Division. Work on trench system as before.	
	4/3/17		3 other ranks, 6 animals + 1 G.S. wagon reported from D.A.C. 58th Div. for transport work. Heavy trench mortar shelling of front line + C.T.'s. Received message from Hd.Q. 174th Inf. Bde (Q.22 of 4/3/17) that front line and section of Coy H.Q. was much damaged by shell fire + asking for assistance in carrying on repairs which was arranged. No. 511 Field Coy R.E. sites with C.R.E. + set out S.P.'s for a garrison of 1 Platoon of Infantry on E + N sides of BELLACOURT and BASSEUX ROAD.	A.A.3.
	"	10.30am	Casualties. 7th Bn L.1 Regt Princess attached. Killed 2 O.R. Wounded 4 O.R. in LIMERICK LANE.	

Army Form C. 2118.

WAR DIARY
or
INTELLIGENCE SUMMARY.
(Erase heading not required.)

571 Field Coy R.E.

Place	Date	Hour	Summary of Events and Information	Remarks and references to Appendices
	5/3/17		Preparing Works on trench system as before.	
BAILLEULMONT			R.E. dump at BAILLEULMONT shelled by the enemy with 4.2" and 5.9" H.E. and Shrapnel shell.	
	6/3/17		No. 3 Field Co. R.E. arranged for repair of damage by shell fire to trenches and by Trafps. Argent at the forward end of LINCOLN LANE. Wire in front of trenches repaired.	
			Change of Front:- (1) Taken over R.E. Supervision of trenches from BOUNDARY POST inclusive to ENGINEER ST and DYKE STREET exclusive with maps, Iclones Yc. relating to the work and R.E. dump. GROSVILLE, to SD 3.20 Field Co R.E.	
			(2) Taken over R.E. Supervision of trench system from 21st STREET inclusive to M.28.d.85.38. in addition to present area. (Ref. Map. 57 D S.E. & 57 C S.W.)	
			(3) 571 Field Co. R.E. went to LA CAUCHIE to discuss with O.C. 92nd Div. First Field Ambulance works required at their camps. Fallen screen on BAILLEULMONT-LA CAUCHIE ROAD was inspected and arrangements made for re-erection. R.E. Camps at BAILLEULMONT shelled.	
	7/3/17		One Sapper Carpenter lent to supervise hut section at LA CAUCHIE for No. 1 H.C. Field Ambulance. Works on trench system as before. No. 3 & 4 Sections and attached Pioneers moved from BAILLEULMONT to BETHEL. Half of No. 3 Section & attached Pioneers moved from BAILLEULMONT to BELLACOURT.	

Army Form C. 2118.

WAR DIARY
or
INTELLIGENCE SUMMARY.
(Erase heading not required.)

511 Field Coy R.E.

Place	Date	Hour	Summary of Events and Information	Remarks and references to Appendices
BAILLEULMONT	8/3/17		Work on trench system as before; heavy shelling, damage to front line and wire.	
	9/3/17		Making dugouts at BAILLEULMONT.	
	9/3/17		Establishment: 2 Other ranks of D.A.C. 58th Divsion reported for duty.	
			1 L.D. horse sent to hospital with mange	
	10/3/17 to 12/3/17		Work on trench system as before; repairing wire.	
	12/3/17		Improving dugouts at BAILLEULMONT.	
			Commander XVIII Corps inspected line from PARK STREET to RENFREW ROAD	
			Improving Prisoners cage, BAILLEULMONT.	
LA CAUCHIE			Particulars taken of platforms required by A.S.C., 17th Bde. Nine Other ranks, 18 animals, and	
BAILLEULMONT	13/3/17 to 15/3/17		3 G.S. wagons of D.A.C. 58th Division returned to Unit.	
			Work on trench system as before. Improving Prisoners cage, BAILLEULMONT.	
	14/3/17		Establishment - 7 Other ranks, 7 animals and 1 G.S. wagon of D.A.C. 58th Division returned to Unit.	
	15/3/17		Works for improved water supply at BAILLEULMONT inspected. Improving Prisoners cage.	
	14/3/17		G.O.C. Third Army, G.O.C. 58th Division and G.O.C. 17th Bde inspected nights of trench system of	
			No left sector. C.R.E. visited left sector. Works on trench system as before.	

Army Form C. 2118.

WAR DIARY
or
INTELLIGENCE SUMMARY.
(Erase heading not required.)

511 Field Coy R.E.

Place	Date	Hour	Summary of Events and Information	Remarks and references to Appendices
BAILLEULMONT	16/3/17		Casualty. 2/Lt Bn 6.1 Regt Pioneers attached; Wounded 1 O.R.	24/18
	17/3/17		Work on Pioneers Camp, BAILLEULMONT. Work on trench system in Wipers slightly hostile artillery activity	7/9/19
	17/3/17 to 18/3/17		Enemy vacated the whole of his front line system of trenches opposite Divisional Front. Roads in enemy lines reconnoitred for repairs required to make them passable for traffic. Company and attached Pioneers employed on making good roads crossing our own and enemy lines into RANSART.	27/18
	19/3/17	3.30pm	Company HQrs moved from BAILLEULMONT to BRETENCOURT and No 2 + 4 Sections with Pioneers moved from BERLES to BRETENCOURT. Party No. 3. Section with half of YYK CLR Pioneers moved from BAILLEULMONT to BELLACOURT. Roads crossing our own and enemy lines made good. One Battalion of Infantry (YKK CLR) also employed in road repairs	11/19
	20/3/17		Whole Company and attached Pioneers employed on repairs to BELLACOURT - RANSART, and FICHEUX - BOISLEUX-AU-MONT - BOISLEUX - ST MARC ROADS	27/19
	27/3/17		Whole of Company with attached Pioneers worked on repairs to roads in accordance with instructions received from CRE 58th Division. Working party furnished by YKA CLR.	7/9/18

Army Form C. 2118

WAR DIARY
or
INTELLIGENCE SUMMARY.
(Erase heading not required.)

511 Field Coy R.E.

Place	Date	Hour	Summary of Events and Information	Remarks and references to Appendices
	27/3/17		Road Repairs as before. Company Headqs. and Nos. 2 & 4 Sections with Pioneers attacked left BRETEN COURT and proceeded to BETLET. Nos. 1 and 3 Sections with attached Pioneers proceeded from BEZENCOURT to ADINFER.	9/19
	28/3/17		Repairs to Roads as before.	9/19
	29/3/17		do with addition of roads in the neighbourhood of BETLET	9/13
	29/3/17		Orders received today from CRE that the Company would move to LUCHEUX on 26th instant.	9/13

F.J. Burwick
Major R.E.
O/c 511 Field Coy

Vol 4

War Diary
of
511 Field Coy R.E.
From 1/4/17 to 25/4/17

Volume III

Army Form C. 2118.

WAR DIARY
INTELLIGENCE SUMMARY
(Erase heading not required.)

511 FIELD COY. R.E.

Instructions regarding War Diaries and Intelligence Summaries are contained in F. S. Regs., Part II. and the Staff Manual respectively. Title pages will be prepared in manuscript.

Place	Date	Hour	Summary of Events and Information	Remarks and references to Appendices
LUCHEUX	1/4/17		Coy HQ, Nos. 1+2 Sections with 75th, 78th, 79th and 79th Pioneers attached, moved from LUCHEUX to LIGNY-SUR-CANCHE.	A15
			Sections 3+4 remained at LUCHEUX for works on rifle range	
LIGNY-SUR-CANCHE	2/4/17		Coy. H.Q., Nos. 1+2 Sections, 75th, 78th, 79th and 79th Pioneers attached, moved from LIGNY-SUR-CANCHE to CHERIENNES.	A18
LUCHEUX	"		Nos. 3+4 Sections moved to BOURQUEMAISON	A18
CHERIENNES	3/4/17		Overhauling wagons, &c, repairing wheels.	A18
"	4/4/17		Nos. 1+2 Sections & all Pioneers attached left CHERIENNES & proceeded by forced stages to LIVRE CAMP, MAILLY-MAILLET.	A19
"	"		Coy HQ. moved from CHERIENNES to AUCHONVILLERS.	
"	"	3 p.m.	Transport Section moved from CHERIENNES to HEM en route to MAILLY-MAILLET	
BOURQUEMAISON	5/4/17	3 p.m.	No. 3 Section proceeded from BOURQUEMAISON and reformed Units at LIVRE CAMP, MAILLY-MAILLET.	A18
"	"		No. 4 Section moved from BOURQUEMAISON to DOMART.	
HEM	"	4.30 pm	Transport completed move from CHERIENNES to MAILLY-MAILLET	
AUCHONVILLERS	6/4/17	10.30 am	Coy HQ. moved from AUCHONVILLERS to LIVRE CAMP, MAILLY-MAILLET	A18
MAILLY-MAILLET	7/4/17		Coy H.Q. Nos. 1, 3+3 Sections and all attached Pioneers left LIVRE CAMP, MAILLY-MAILLET and	A18 / 298

WAR DIARY
INTELLIGENCE SUMMARY

(2)

Army Form C. 2118.

511 FIELD COY. R.E.

Place	Date	Hour	Summary of Events and Information	Remarks and references to Appendices
MAILLY-MAILLET	7/4/17		Proceeded to Camp on North Side of the BIHUCOURT-SAPIGNIES ROAD near ACHIET-LE-GRAND (Map ref:- 57.c N.W. G.12.d.2.7)	A.J.R
BIHUCOURT	8/4/17		Works and improving Camp	A.J.R
"	9/4/17		Repairing, maintaining & draining roads:- ERVILLERS-MORY; making Subsidiary round crater at ECOUST	A.J.R
"	10/4/17		-do- :- ERVILLERS-MORY, ERVILLERS-ST LEGER, ERVILLERS-ECOUST, and MORY-VRAUCOURT.	A.J.R
"	11/4/17 to 14/4/17		Casualty:- 1 other rank accidentally injured whilst on duty. Repairs on roads, as before; filling in shell holes.	A.J.R
"	15/4/17 to 17/4/17		Repairs on roads, as before; filling in shell holes on VRAUCOURT-SUGRETTE ROAD and repairing round pound crater	A.J.R
	18/4/17		Instructing Infantry in Trusty wire entanglement	A.J.R
	20/4/17		Repairs on roads, filling shell holes:- MORY-ECOUST, ERVILLERS-MORY. Instructing Infantry in Trusty wiring	A.J.R
	22/4/17		No.4 Section moved from DOMART to TOUTENCOURT.	A.J.R

Army Form C. 2118.

WAR DIARY

INTELLIGENCE SUMMARY. 511 FIELD COY. R.E.

(Erase heading not required.)

Place	Date	Hour	Summary of Events and Information	Remarks and references to Appendices
BIHUCOURT	2/4/17 to		No. 1. Section :- Engineer training.	A.9.R
			Nos 2 & 3 Sections :- Repairs & maintenance of MORY-ÉCOUST and ST LEGER-VRAUCOURT	
	29/4/17		ROAD. Instructing Infantry in wiring	

J.P. Spencer, Major R.E.
Commd. 511 Field Co. R.E.

Army Form C. 2118.

WAR DIARY

~~INTELLIGENCE~~ SUMMARY.

(Erase heading not required.)

5/1st FIELD COY R.E.

Place	Date	Hour	Summary of Events and Information	Remarks and references to Appendices
Reference Map 57c N.W.	26/4/17		Repairing and maintaining MORY–ÉCOUST ROAD (Br. 622 to Écoust). Filling in shell holes. Carrying out and forming team.	A.9.S
	24/4/17		All Pioneers of 25th, 27th, 28th and 29th Bn. Londen Regt returned to their respective Units.	A.9.S
	27/4/17 & 28/4/17		Nos. 2 & 3 Sections:– Repairs to MORY–ÉCOUST ROAD in Ecoust. Pumping out and filling. No.1 mine craters.	A.9.S
	29/4/17		No.1 Section: Engineering training. Instruction in cavity mine entanglements. Two 1st & 3 Sections: Repairs to MORY–ÉCOUST ROAD; Pumping out and filling No. 1 mine craters, making diversion round No. 2 mine crater.	A.9.S
	30/4/17		Nos. 1 & 3 Sections: Repairs & maintenance of MORY–ÉCOUST ROAD in Ecoust. No. 2 Section: Engineer training; instruction in cavity mine entanglements	A.9.S

J.J. Lyman
Major R.E.(?)
Commd: 5/1st Field Coy R.E.

WAR DIARY

INTELLIGENCE SUMMARY

511th FIELD COY. R.E.

Army Form C. 2118.

Place	Date	Hour	Summary of Events and Information	Remarks and references to Appendices
Map Ref:— 57.C N.N	1/5/17 & 2/5/17		Sections 1 & 3:- Repair and maintenance of MORY-ECOUST ROAD (L'ABBAYE to ECOUST); Filling in shell holes. No 1 Section: making division sump. No 2 Section: To 2 Bn Gtr. Engineer Training.	J.J.S.
	2/5/17 3/5/17		Instructions received from CRE 58th Division to prepare to move on 3/5/17 (No H 2/5/17) Sections 1, 2 & 3: Repairs & maintenance of MORY-ECOUST ROAD, as before, & returned to own lines after work.	J.J.S.
	4/5/17		Company HQrs moved from Camp between BIHUCOURT and SAPIGNIES and proceeded to Camp at B.23.c.72.10. (Map Ref 57.D. N.W.) between MORY & VRAUX-VRAUCOURT. Received orders from CRE 58th Division that Company would commence training from 5/5/17.	J.J.S.
	5/5/17		No 1 & 2 Sections with 1 & 3 Section:- Repair of MORY-ECOUST ROAD as before. No 3 Section (half):- Improvement of water supply at MORY. Physical training, squad & company drill; setting up benches at night; examining tools in carts and pack saddles; testing apparatus, cleaning and examining harness.	J.J.S.

Army Form C. 2118.

Army Form C. 2118.

WAR DIARY
INTELLIGENCE SUMMARY
(Erase heading not required.)

511th Field Company R.E.

Place	Date	Hour	Summary of Events and Information	Remarks and references to Appendices
Reference Map 57c N.W.	6/5/17		Company training:- Physical training; squad & Company drill; setting out strong points at night; wiring on day and at night; fitting of harness; inspection of adjustment of mounted men harness.	A.9.S
	7/5/17		Company in training:- Physical training; explosives and fitting up Bangalore Torpedoes; exploding torpedoes at night; setting out strong points at night. Lecture to Mounted section on care & management of horses.	A.9.S
	8/5/17		Company in training:- Physical training; schemes for defence of woods and villages; wiring at night; explosives and fitting up Bangalore Torpedoes and exploding same at night; riding and driving drill.	A.9.S
	9/5/17		Company in training:- Physical training; pontoon & trestle bridging; lecture; riding & driving drill	A.9.S
	10/5/17		Company in training:- Route march	A.9.S
	11/5/17		Field training with 174th Infantry Brigade, comprising construction of Strong Points at G 34 b 2.7 and G 34 d.7.9; clearing away wire & bridging trenches; clearing roads on N.W. side of LOUPART WOOD & between points G.28.d.7.9 and G.34.b.2.7. Received instructions from C.R.E. 58th Division to take over on 13/5/17 from 503rd Field Co. R.E. work in hand.	A.9.S
	12/5/17	11 am	Inspection of Company by C.R.E. 58th Division. Party of 1 officer & 8 O.R. proceeded to Fifth Army Rest Camp, ST VALERY-SUR-SOMME. Camp shelled by enemy.	A.9.S

Army Form C. 2118.

WAR DIARY
INTELLIGENCE SUMMARY
(Erase heading not required.)

57th Field Company R.E.

Place	Date	Hour	Summary of Events and Information	Remarks and references to Appendices
Reference Map 57°.N.N	13/3/17		Took over from 503rd Field Co. R.E. work in hand:-	
			No.1 Section:- ACHIET-LE-GRAND - BIHUCOURT - BIEFVILLERS Overland track:- cutting road through houses etc, cutting ramp at road crossings: ACHIET-LE-GRAND - BEHAGNIES Overland Track - levelling ground: MIRAUMONT Salvage Dump - supervising loading of material.	
			No.2 Section:- VRAUCOURT - ECOUST Road - filling in Crater.	
			No.3 Section:- MORY - ECOUST Road (B.17 & 2.3):- Widening cross roads: SAPIGNIES - VRAUCOURT Overland track:- BEHAGNIES - MORY - L'HOMME MORT Overland Track - improving forward end.	F.J.B
			No.1 Section proceeded to Camp on BIHUCOURT - SAPIGNIES Road.	
	14/3/17		No.1 Section:- ACHIET-LE-GRAND - BIHUCOURT - BIEFVILLERS Overland Tracks:- filling shell holes, marking out route, clearing some + preparing posts for making track: ACHIET-LE-GRAND - BEHAGNIES Overland track - levelling track. MIRAUMONT Salvage Dump - supervising loading of material.	
			Nos 2 + 3 Sections: Work as on previous day. Work of No.2 Section considerably interfered with by heavy shelling.	F.J.B
			Instructions received from O.R.E 56th Division to take over work from 51st Field Co. R.E.	
			Camp shelled by enemy.	

WAR DIARY

INTELLIGENCE SUMMARY

(Erase heading not required.)

Army Form C. 2118.

511th Field Company. R.E.

Place	Date	Hour	Summary of Events and Information	Remarks and references to Appendices
Reference Map 57° N.W	15/5/17		O.C. conferred with O.C 511th Field Co R.E. as to taking over work of that Company.	
			No. 1 Section - ACHIET-LE-GRAND - BIHUCOURT - BIEFVILLERS Overland track - filling in shell holes, filling in trench, cutting away verge, preparing pickets. MIRAUMONT Salvage Dump - selecting material.	A.J.18.
			No. 2 Section - Work as on previous day.	
			No. 3 Section - MORY-ECOUST Road - widening cross roads and Behagnies road. ERVILLERS - MORY Overland Track - making ramp at B.21.b.05.40. BEHAGNIES - MORY Overland Track - improving forward end.	
	16/5/17		No. 1 Section. ACHIET-LE-GRAND - BIHUCOURT - BIEFVILLERS Overland Track - laying out & improving track.	
			No. 2 Section. VRAUCOURT - ECOUST Road - filling in crater (work interfered with by enemy gas shells).	A.J.18
			No. 3 Section Work as in Camp.	
			Took over from 511th Field Co. R.E. work in BULLECOURT area.	
			Roads into BULLECOURT reconnoitred with C.R.E 58th Division.	
	17/5/17		No. 1 Section. Laying out & improving Overland Tracks, ACHIET-LE-GRAND - BIHUCOURT - BIEFVILLERS + ACHIET-LE-GRAND - BEHAGNIES.	
			No. 3 Section ERVILLERS - MORY Overland Track - Digging ramp at forward end, ST LEGER - VRAUCOURT. Digging 2nd Line Defence Line Trench.	A.J.18
			6. O.R. 2/7th Battalion London Regt. attached for duty at R.E. Dump, MORY.	

WAR DIARY

~~INTELLIGENCE SUMMARY.~~   511th Field Company R.E.

Army Form C. 2118.

(Erase heading not required.)

Instructions regarding War Diaries and Intelligence Summaries are contained in F.S. Regs, Part II. and the Staff Manual respectively. Title pages will be prepared in manuscript.

Place	Date	Hour	Summary of Events and Information	Remarks and references to Appendices
Reference Map 57d N.W.	17/5/17		OC examined ground for Communication Trench to be constructed in BULLECOURT	F.S.18.
			No. 2 Section proceeded to work on construction of Strong Point on W. side of BULLECOURT (U.27.b. 37.75)	
	18/5/17		No. 1 Section. Work as on previous day. Work in hand by No.1 Section handed over to 500th Field	
			Co. R.E. No.1 Section returned to Camp at B.23.c. 72.10	
			OC visited G.O.C. 174th Brigade	F.S.18.
			No. 2 Section - Construction of Strong Point, BULLECOURT, at Point U.27.b. 35.75.	
			No. 3 Section: BULLECOURT AVENUE C.T. - Cleaning & improving trench and laying trench boards.	
	19/5/17		Captain NEWTON & Lieut. LACE met Officers of 290th Bde R.F.A. with reference to construction of O.Ps	A.V.18.
			No. 4 Section returned to Unit from Fifth Army School of Instruction, TOUTENCOURT.	
			No. 1 Section - BULLECOURT AVENUE C.T. (C.3.0.3.1. to C.8.b.6.6.) Deepening trench	
			No. 2 Section - BULLECOURT S.P. - Lengthening right flank & completing wiring of Strong Point.	
			No. 3 Section - BULLECOURT AVENUE C.T. - Deepening trench and laying trench boards.	
	20/5/17		2nd Lieut. J.T. BARING slightly wounded.	
			No. 3 Section (under O.B.) - BULLECOURT AVENUE C.T. - Deepening & improving trench. Construction of	F.S.18.
			Signallers' Dugout for C. Battery, 290th Brigade R.F.A. at (approximately) B.12 central.	
			No. 4 Section - BULLECOURT AVENUE C.T. (towards S.W.) - Deepening and improving trench	

WAR DIARY

INTELLIGENCE SUMMARY

Army Form C. 2118.

511th Field Company R.E.

Place	Date	Hour	Summary of Events and Information	Remarks and references to Appendices
Reference Map 51° N.W.	20/5/17		No. 4 Section (cont) - Construction of O.P. for A Battery, 290th Bde R.F.A. at Point C.3.c.40. Digging new C.T. along Ecoust-Noreuil Road from C.2.d.3.5. to Bullecourt Avenue.	F.J.B.
	21/5/17		No. 1 Section stood by in the line at disposal of Brigadier 174th Brigade in connection with attack on Bovis Trench; attack unsuccessful; section returned to camp. Nos. 2 & 3 Sections - Bullecourt Avenue C.T. - deepening and improving trench. No. 4 Section - C.2.d.8.5. to Bullecourt Avenue - Deepening & improving new C.T. along Ecoust-Noreuil Road. O.C. discussed work in hand with C.R.E. 58th Division at his office. 1 Officer's Rider and 1 Rider received as remounts.	F.J.B.
	22/5/17		No. 1 Section - C.2.d.8.5. to Bullecourt Avenue - widening trench and laying trench boards. Bullecourt Avenue (extension towards S.W.) - clearing & deepening trench & extending to dead ground. Nos. 2 & 4 Sections Bullecourt Avenue C.T. - clearing, deepening & widening trench; improving forward end and laying trench boards. Inspection of animals by A.D.V.S. 58th Division. Camp area shelled by hostile artillery. Casualties: Killed 1 O.R., wounded 3 O.R. (whilst proceeding to works)	F.J.B.
	23/5/17		No. 1 Section - Excavating for C.T. through Bullecourt.	F.J.B.

WAR DIARY
INTELLIGENCE SUMMARY.

511th Field Company. R.E.

Army Form C. 2118.

Place	Date	Hour	Summary of Events and Information	Remarks and references to Appendices
Reference Map 57c N.W.	23/5/17 (contd)		No. 3 Section. Bullecourt Avenue C.T. - Deepening & widening forward end; laying trench boards. Bullecourt Avenue (Centre Section) - Widening trench and laying trench boards. No. 4 Section - Bullecourt Avenue C.T. - making berm; C.2.a.8.5. to Bullecourt Avenue - widening and deepening trench; laying trench boards. O.C. visited Brigadier, 175th Brigade, at Advanced Brigade Headquarters, The Cave, Ecoust, with regard to work in hand.	J.J.R.
	24/5/17		Burial of Sapper Froud, F., at Mory Military Cemetery (B.22.a.8.7). No. 1 Section. Digging new C.T. through Bullecourt. No. 2 Section. Bullecourt Avenue C.T. (rear area) - Deepening, widening and improving trench. No. 3 Section. Bullecourt Avenue C.T. (forward area) - Deepening, widening and improving trench and laying trench boards. C.R.E. 58th Division visited camp. O.C. visited Brigadier, 175th Brigade at Ecoust and discussed work to be carried out in Bullecourt Area.	J.J.R.
	25/5/17		No. 4 Section - Erection of huts at Headquarters 58th Division. Mory.	J.J.R.

WAR DIARY

INTELLIGENCE SUMMARY

Army Form C. 2118.

Place	Date	Hour	Summary of Events and Information	Remarks and references to Appendices
Map Reference 57c N.W.	25/5/17		No. 2 Section:- Digging new C.T. through BULLECOURT. Party shelled out at 1.30. a.m. No. 3 Section:- BULLECOURT AVENUE C.T.- deepening, widening and improving trench (work very much hampered by heavy shelling of trench) C.2.d.8.5 to BULLECOURT AVENUE - along ECOUST-NOREUIL Road - Deepening and widening trench (work interfered with by shell fire) Casualties - 1 O.R. slightly wounded.	A 913

J.J. Popwater
Major R.E. (T.)
Commdg. 511th Field Co. R.E.

Army Form C. 2118.

WAR DIARY

~~INTELLIGENCE~~ SUMMARY

(Erase heading not required.)

511 FIELD COY. R.E.

Instructions regarding War Diaries and Intelligence Summaries are contained in F. S. Regs., Part II. and the Staff Manual respectively. Title pages will be prepared in manuscript.

Place	Date	Hour	Summary of Events and Information	Remarks and references to Appendices
Reference Map 57c N.W. BULLECOURT	26/5/17		Company HQrs moved to camp at H.3. N.9.0. Two reinforcements arrived from BASE. Three horses evacuated to Mobile Veterinary Section. Setting out & erecting huts at Advanced Divl Hdqrs. Deepening, widening and cleaning trench and laying trench boards C.2. d.8.5 to BULLECOURT AVENUE. Digging new C.T. from BULLECOURT AVENUE eastward along entrenchment in U.28.c.d. Forming up of rifle pits. N.B. visited all works in progress.	J.9.S.
"	27/5/17 to 29/5/17		Work to trenches, as before; deepening + widening BULLECOURT AVENUE C.T.; digging new trench & widening + extending C.T. through BULLECOURT. Erecting huts at Advanced D.H.Q.	J.9.S.
"	27/5/17		Party of 1 Officer & 8 O.R. returned from Fifth Army Rest Camp. One N.C.O. proceeded to — do —	J.9.S.
"	29/5/17		Improving Prisoners' Cage MORY. For I.D. Horses arrived from Remounts.	J.9.S.
"	30/5/17		Deepening & widening BULLECOURT AVENUE C.T., laying trench boards. Superintending carrying of pickets & wire to support line. One O.R. reported as reinforcement from BASE.	J.9.S.
"	31/5/17		Erecting huts at Advanced D.H.Q. Erecting barbed wire entanglements in front of	J.9.S.

Army Form C. 2118.

WAR DIARY
or
INTELLIGENCE SUMMARY.
(Erase heading not required.)

511 Field Coy. R.E.

Place	Date	Hour	Summary of Events and Information	Remarks and references to Appendices
BULLECOURT	3/5/17		Railway Embankment south of BULLECOURT. Widening BULLECOURT AVENUE C.T. Assisting Infantry to make posts on O.G. trench on east side of BULLECOURT.	J.J.R.

F.J. Reynolds
Major RE(?)
Commdg. 511 Field Coy RE

WAR DIARY

INTELLIGENCE SUMMARY

Army Form C. 2118.

571 Field Co RE Vol 6

Place	Date	Hour	Summary of Events and Information	Remarks and references to Appendices
Map Ref. 57cNW.	1/6/17		Assisting Infantry to erect barbed wire entanglements in front of RAILWAY TRENCH, BULLECOURT. Deepening & widening RAILWAY TRENCH, ready for shelters. Improving carrying of material. Deepening Old German trench East of BULLECOURT and improving posts. Erecting huts at Advanced Hqrs. Widening BULLECOURT AVENUE C.T. One officer admitted casualty slightly status (sick).	A.18.
"	2/6/17		Widening BULLECOURT AVENUE C.T.; assisting Infantry to erect barbed wire entanglements in front of RAILWAY TRENCH, S. of BULLECOURT. Excavating to new C.T. from Old German trench at U.17.d.5.4. onwards to forward fire. Putting in fire steps & generally improving posts (BULLECOURT FORWARD POSTS). Deepening BULLECOURT AVENUE C.T. across road, laying duck boards, raising parapets along road to from screen to trench. Erecting & repairing huts at Advanced trot Hqrs. Widening & deepening BULLECOURT AVENUE C.T. Deepening & widening RAILWAY TRENCH, making firesteps & fixing elephant shelters. Killed. 1 O.R. Wounded 1 O.R.	A.18.

WAR DIARY
INTELLIGENCE SUMMARY
(Erase heading not required.)

Army Form C. 2118.

511 FIELD COY R.E.

Place	Date	Hour	Summary of Events and Information	Remarks and references to Appendices
BULLECOURT	3/6/17		Arrivals:- One Sapper as reinforcement.	
	4/6/17		Erecting barbed wire entanglements in front of Railway Embankment trench, East of BULLECOURT. Excavating new C.T. from O.G. trench at U.27.d.5.4. Northwards to Forward Posts. Deepening O.G. trench E. of BULLECOURT, & making Fire bays. Erecting elephant dugouts in right forward Posts, BULLECOURT. Widening & deepening BULLECOURT AVENUE C.T. Deepening & widening RAILWAY EMBANKMENT TRENCH & making fire steps. Erecting Two Advanced Divil. Hdqrs. Mr. Farmed over works to trench system at BULLECOURT to 503rd Field Co. R.E.	T.I.R.
"	5/6/17		Took over works to roads from 503rd Field Co. R.E. Erecting driving norms. Having same, repairing up rd. to Bokko. MORY. Erecting sign-post at Cross Roads, MORY. Repairing MORY-ECOUST Rd. Repairing rd. Filling in crater at B.22.c.1.3. Clearing Mains between MORY + FAVREUIL. (FAVREUIL ROAD.) Making fame, excavating for dugout to be used as Dressing Station at L'HOMME MORT. Supervising cartage of stone for repairs of MORY-ECOUST and SUCRÉRIE ROADS. Erecting tents and making latrines at vicinity of Camp. Shelled. Air bombs dropped near camp by aircraft.	T.I.R.

Army Form C. 2118.

WAR DIARY
INTELLIGENCE SUMMARY.
(Erase heading not required.)

5/11th FIELD COY R.E.

(3)

Place	Date	Hour	Summary of Events and Information	Remarks and references to Appendices
Map Ref 57c NW.	6/6/17		Tracing rebounds & making new road for ASC dump at B.21.a.3.6. Excavating for dugout to be made into dressing station at L'HOMME MORT. Finishing preparation of frame. Erecting new dressing room at Battn. M.O.R.Y. Repairing MORY-ECOUST & MORY-VRAUCOURT ROADS. Filling in craters at MORY at B.22.c.1.3 (FAVREUIL ROAD). Blowing drains & repairing MORY-FAVREUIL ROAD. Supervising cartage of stone for repairs of MORY-ECOUST & SUCRERIE ROADS.	7.1.18.
	7/6/17		Completing excavation & erecting frames at Dressing Station, L'HOMME MORT. Making up new road for ASC dump at B.21.a.3.6. with broken brick. Filling in shell-holes & generally repairing roads (overland tracks), as follows :- VRAUCOURT-SAPIGNIES-BIHUCOURT, MORY-BEHAGNIES-ACHIET LE GRAND, MORY-ERVILLERS, MORY-BIHUCOURT. Erecting new dressing room at the Battn. MORY. Repairing MORY-ECOUST, MORY-FAVREUIL and VRAUCOURT-ECOUST ROADS. Filling in craters at B.22.c.1.3 (FAVREUIL RD). Supervising cartage of stone for repair of SUCRERIE-ECOUST RD. Supervising Infantry at R.E. training.	7.1.18.

WAR DIARY
INTELLIGENCE SUMMARY

Army Form C. 2118.

511 FIELD COY RE

Place	Date	Hour	Summary of Events and Information	Remarks and references to Appendices
Map Ref. 57 C. N.M.	8/4/17		Arrivals:- 6 O.R. from No 4 Reinforcement Coy RE. Erecting mires frame at Dressing Station, L'HOMME MORT. Making up wire broken tried net road to ASC dump at B.21.a.3.b. Filling shell holes & ruts & generally repairing overland tracks as yesterday. Erecting lath houses MORY. Repairing wire netting in crater as yesterday. Making latrines at Advanced Dsg. Stn. Making & erecting camouflage screens on MORY-ECOUST ROAD at C.2.d.6.7. Supervising getting of stone to repair 4 roads. Instructing Infantry of 25th 76th & 219th Bn C.L.R. in R.E. training by day & at night.	A.918
	9/4/17		Building double roof to dugout at L'HOMME MORT to be used as Dressing Station. Making up wire broken tried new road to ASC Dump at B.21.a.3.b. Repairing VRAUCOURT-SAPIGNIES-BIHUCOURT overland track. Supervising cartage of stone for repairs of MORY-ECOUST and SUCRERIE-ECOUST ROADS. Repairing the following roads:- MORY-ECOUST, MORY-FAVREUIL, VRAUCOURT-ECOUST. Filling in crater at B.22.c.1.3. (FAVREUIL ROAD). Erecting shed at Adv. Dsg. Stn.	A.R.

Army Form C. 2118.

WAR DIARY
or
INTELLIGENCE SUMMARY.
(Erase heading not required.)

511th Field Coy. R.E

Instructions regarding War Diaries and Intelligence Summaries are contained in F. S. Regs., Part II. and the Staff Manual respectively. Title pages will be prepared in manuscript.

Place	Date	Hour	Summary of Events and Information	Remarks and references to Appendices
Map Ref. 57c NW	9/6/17		Making & erecting camouflage screens at C.2.d.6.9. (ÉCOUST). Instructing three Battalions of Infantry etc in R.E. Training.	A.9.18
	10/6/17		Ten O.R. proceeded to Rest Camp (left army). One O.R. returned for this Rest Camp. Building up double roof to dugout of L'HOMME MORT Dressing Station. Making up with stones broken new road at NSC dump at B.21.a.3.6. Supervising cartage of stone for repair of MORY-ÉCOUST & SUCRERIE-ÉCOUST ROADS. Repairing the following roads:— MORY-FAVREUIL, MORY-ÉCOUST, and VRAUCOURT-ÉCOUST. Filling in craters at B.22. C.1.3. (FAVREUIL RD.) Clearing out ditch along MORY-FAVREUIL ROAD (B.22 C. to B.21.d.) Making latrines at R.E. Dump MORT. Supervising 75th Batn. C.L.R. in R.E. training at night.	A.1.18
"	11/6/17		Drawing stores at L'HOMME MORT & RPA. Revoking NSC sand-bagging entrance. Making lecture terraces to carry cyclopedia. New road 15 NSC dump. Completed. Making lectures rooms & distribution at L'HOMME MORT and Lower ÉCOUST & NOREUIL. Supervising loading & distribution of metal on MORY-ÉCOUST & VRAUCOURT-ÉCOUST ROADS. Instructing NCR Batn. O.R. in consolidation of shell holes. Shoring up building in FAVREUIL for 1/2 A.C. Field Ambulance. Repairing roads & filling in crater at R.E. Dump	A.9.18

WAR DIARY

INTELLIGENCE SUMMARY
(Erase heading not required.)

Army Form C. 2118.

511 FIELD COY RE

Place	Date	Hour	Summary of Events and Information	Remarks and references to Appendices
Map Ref. 57c NW	11/4/17		Clearing out with [?] areas of MORY in direction of ERVILLERS. Excavating for latrines & privy seats at ECOUST. Repairing latrine seats at RE Rifle Pits.	A.9.18
	12/4/17		Repairing at RE dumps, MORT. Timber for doors at B.21.d.85.30. Laying planks, dugout & trench grid to approach of advising station for R.F.A. at L'HOMME MORT. Making res-road for RSC Dump as yesterday. Improving siding & destruction of road metal on MORY-ECOUST and VRAUCOURT-ECOUST ROADS. Making trench screens & camouflage road from level near MORY dump to L'HOMME MORT. Firing vertical trestling shores to building occupied by 2 H.C.F.A. at ERVILLERS. Repairing roads as yesterday. Clearing out ditch on West side of MORY in the direction of ERVILLERS. Making latrine seats as at RE dumps MORT. Filling in crater in MORY at B22.C.1.3 (FAVREUIL RD.) 2 O.R. proceeded to V Corps school VAUCHELLES for duty.	A.9.19
"	13/4/17		Excavating & fixing six chevaux de MORY cross roads (B21.d T.30) Improving, loading & distributing road metal on MORY-ECOUST ROAD. Making & fixing camouflage screens as yesterday. Shoring walls, fixing spanish trestles to R.F. Tunnel on building at ERVILLERS occupied by 2/2 H.C. Field Ambulance	A.9.18.

WAR DIARY

INTELLIGENCE SUMMARY

Army Form C. 2118.

511 FIELD COY RE

Place	Date	Hour	Summary of Events and Information	Remarks and references to Appendices
Map Ref. 57c NW	13/6/17		Filling in craters in MORY at B.22 c.1.3. Clearing, deepening & improving ditch west of MORY to MORY to JEVILLERS, clearing away excavated mud & rubbish. Cleaning, deepening & improving ditch in MORY in B.21. d. 85.80. Repairing roads as yesterday. Erecting latrines in camps of 31st batt of Yorks Regt.	4.9.18
"	14/6/17		Fixing wire netting, netting approaches trenching posts to MORY loops roads at B.21. d. 85.80. Distributing road metal along MORY-ECOUST Rd. Making, erecting trenching screens to camouflage road from MORY to L'HOMME MORT. Moving building acquired by the 7th Field Ambulance & starting another. Filling in crater at MORY as before. Cleaning, ditches & repairing roads as yesterday. Strengthening & improving light railway bridge over ditch at B.21. d. 85. 80. Erecting latrines in camp of 31st C.L.R.	4.9.18
"	15/6/17		Clearing up debris of MORY, making same as before. Filling in water as MORY & improving roads as previously. Erecting screens for camouflaging road from L'HOMME MORT to ECOUST. Erecting Elephant Shelter at D.H.Q.	4.9.18
BULLECOURT	16/6/17		Handed over all works in hand to 503 Field Coy R.E. Took over from 503 Field Coy R.E. all R.E. work in BULLECOURT. (Map Ref 57c NW) systems at BULLECOURT in connection with French.	4.9.R

WAR DIARY

Army Form C. 2118.

(8) 511th Field Coy. R.E.

Instructions regarding War Diaries and Intelligence Summaries are contained in F.S. Regs., Part II. and the Staff Manual respectively. Title pages will be prepared in manuscript.

Place	Date	Hour	Summary of Events and Information	Remarks and references to Appendices
BULLECOURT Map Ref. 57cNW	16/6/17		Front line trench from U.22.c.45.10 to U.22.c.30.15 :— Deepening & improving subways trench behind parapets. — Towards end of Bullecourt Avenue (HACKNEY MATCHES):— Deepening & widening trench. — Gordon Switch Line.— Deepening widening trench, building sand-bag wall behind M.G.E.— Front trench in U.28.b. and U.29.a.— Deepening front line trench, filling sand-bags for traverses & firesteps.— TANK AVENUE (U.28.a.):— forming fire bays (east side of firesteps.) TANK AVENUE. RAILWAY TRENCH (from U.27.d.15.55. to U.23.d.0.15.):— Deepening, widening & improving trench, excavating for firestep. Arrivals:— 1.O.R.	J.9.18.
"	17/6/17		Work to RAILWAY TRENCH & TANK AVENUE as yesterday. Deepening LONDON TRENCH to right and left of TANK AVENUE. Work to Front line trench + GORDON SWITCH, as before. Casualties:— 1.O.R. wounded (at duty)	J.9.18.
"	18/6/17		Handed over works at BULLECOURT to 9th Field Co. R.E. and took over work to trench system at left of BULLECOURT from 504 Field Co. RE. Deepening & improving RAILWAY TRENCH from U.27.d.0.65. to U.25.d.0.15. & reverting firesteps.	J.9.18.

Army Form C. 2118.

WAR DIARY

INTELLIGENCE SUMMARY ~~~ 511 FIELD COY R.E.

(Erase heading not required.)

Instructions regarding War Diaries and Intelligence Summaries are contained in F. S. Regs., Part II. and the Staff Manual respectively. Title pages will be prepared in manuscript.

Place	Date	Hour	Summary of Events and Information	Remarks and references to Appendices
Map Ref. 57C N.W.	18/6/17		Repairing track of light railway from MORY-ECOUST. Setting out & excavating for the following Strong Points:- No.1 at U.20.b.4.2, No.2 at U.20.b.2.5, No.3 at U.20.a.9.9. and No.4 at U.14.c.25.95. Deepening LONDON TRENCH on the west side of junction with TANK AVENUE. Improving existing freelays to GORDON SWITCH (BULLECOURT), and excavating for additional tr.	F.9.1.8
"	19/6/17		Tracing new C.T. from U.19.b.9.8. to U.14.c.7.t. Digging new C.T. from U.21.c.0.40. to U.20.d.60.75. Digging fire trenches and making traverses to S.Ps. No.1,2,3 & 4. Casualties:- 1.O.R.	F.9.1.8
"	20/6/17		Arrival: 1.O.R. Deepening forward end of PELICAN and S.Ps.	F.9.1.8
"	21/6/17 & 27/6/17		Work to new C.T's as yesterday, and S.Ps as yesterday. 2 Officers reported for duty on 21/6/17. AVENUE C.T.	F.9.1.8
"	22/6/17		Work to C.T.'s + S.P's as before.	F.9.1.8
"	23/6/17		1.O.R. killed. Work to C.T's + S.P's as before. Handed over works on hand to 528 Field Co R.E. Company resting.	F.9.1.8
"	24/6/17		Whole of Company moved from H.3.b.90. to A.21.b.3.9. (COURCELLES-Le-COMTE)	F.9.1.8

WAR DIARY

(10) Army Form C. 2118.

511 Field Co. R.E.

Place	Date	Hour	Summary of Events and Information	Remarks and references to Appendices
Map Ref. 57c NW	24/6/17		Arrival:- 1 O.R.	
	25/6/17		Improving new camp at COURCELLES. Inspector of Rifles gave helmets to Infantry & R.E.	A.9.8
	26/6/17 to 30/6/17		Training of Company. Instructing 16 Officers & 258 O.R. Infantry of 174th Brigade in R.E. training	
	30/6/17		Arrivals: 1 Officer	

F.V. Ryworth
Major R.E.
Comdt 511 Field Co. R.E.

Vol 7

Army Form C. 2118.

511 Field Company R.E.

WAR DIARY

INTELLIGENCE SUMMARY.
(Erase heading not required.)

Instructions regarding War Diaries and Intelligence Summaries are contained in F.S. Regs., Part II. and the Staff Manual respectively. Title pages will be prepared in manuscript.

Place	Date	Hour	Summary of Events and Information	Remarks and references to Appendices
Hdq Bn 5Y.C	1-7-17		Church Parade. Instructing Infantry of 174th Inf. Bde in simple R.E. work	A.9.S.
	2/7/17 to 3/7/17		Instructing Infantry as yesterday. R.E. training of Company.	A.9.S.
	4/7/17		Advance party of 9.O.R. proceeded to METZ-en-COUTURE (Q.20.c.). R.E. training of Company and Instructing Infantry in R.E. work.	A.9.S.
	5/7/17		Short route march; dismantling training works.	A.9.S.
	6/7/17	4 p.m.	Reinforcements:- 1.O.R. & H. L.D. Forest. Clearing up and leaving camp at COURCELLES-le-COMTE (A.21.k.3.9). No. 1 Company moved from COURCELLES to camp at BARCOURT (H.36.d.)	A.9.S.
	7/7/17	4.30pm	No.2 Company moved from BARCOURT to EQUANCOURT (V.10.b.39.)	A.9.S.
	8/7/17		No.3, No.4 Co's &6 & 7 & 70 Field Coys R.E. re taking over new line (Q.5.a.4.9 to R.7.b.7.3.) Repairing well & pump at SUGAR FACTORY, METZ.	A.9.S.
	9/7/17		No. 2nd G.O.C. 174th Brigade, at DESSART WOOD and CRE at YPRES about R.E. work in this Sector. Company with exception of Mounted Section moved from EQUANCOURT to METZ-en-COUTURE (Q.20.c.6.7). Took over line in this Sector from #67 & 470 Field Coys R.E. Repairing well & pump at SUGAR FACTORY, METZ.	A.9.S.

WAR DIARY

INTELLIGENCE SUMMARY
(Erase heading not required.)

Army Form C. 2118.

511 Field Coy. R.E.

Place	Date	Hour	Summary of Events and Information	Remarks and references to Appendices
Maps Ref 57c	10/7/17		Deepening LEICESTER & SHAFTESBURY AVENUES (C.T.'s); deepening & laying trench tramway to LINCOLN LANE C.T. Repairing well & fixing engine & pump at SUGAR FACTORY, METZ. Doing & assembling materials at R.E. Dump, METZ. Widening & repairing billets. Reinforcements:- 1 O.R.	A.J.R.
	11/7/17		R.E. supervision of Infantry Working Parties on following works:- Excavating for & improving frames for R.A.P. dugout, Left Batn. Excavating for & fixing small shelters in Front Line, Left Batn, and Coy. Hdqrs, Support Line. Deepening, widening & improving LEICESTER AVENUE and LINCOLN AVENUE C.T.'s. Widening & improving BATH COMP P. SWITCH. Deepening & improving near F. & forward ends of SHAFTESBURY AVENUE C.T. Improving drainage of Intermediate Line & digging sumps &c.	A.J.R.
	12/7/17		1 O.R. proceeded to England to take up R.E. commission; 1 O.R. admitted hospital. Improving billets at METZ. Making frames for front line shelters at R.E. Dump, METZ.	A.J.R.
	13/7/17		Work as yesterday. Making trench gates & shelter frames at R.E. dump, METZ. Excavating for & fixing splinterproof shelters for R.D.S. at Q.21.a.3.6. Taking down and erecting huts and elephant shelters for 174th Brigade Hdqrs.	A.J.R.
	14/7/17		Works & trenches as before.	A.J.R.

WAR DIARY

Army Form C. 2118.

511 Field Company R.E. (3)

Place	Date	Hour	Summary of Events and Information	Remarks and references to Appendices
Map Ref. 57c	15/7/17		Work to trenches as before. Deepening & widening LINCOLN LANE C.T. Excavating for & erecting shelter for AAMC at Q.23.a.8.2. Erecting shelter huts for Table Top.	A.1.A.
	16/7/17		Work as yesterday. Laying floor & RAP dugout. Excavating for shelter in Front Line, Left Bn. & erecting shelters for ADS at Q.21.b.3.b. Deepening & widening Front Line trench, Left Batt. to Table Trench gates. Making trench notice boards. Bomb cases &c. at RE dump, METZ. Fixing pumping engine & connecting up pumps at SUGAR FACTORY, METZ.	A.9.A.
	17/7/17		Finished over mantle on Hythe Brigade Stoves (from Pyt.7.2 to Q.5.a.9.1.) to 5th Field Coy. R.E. Work High Level trench bridges as yesterday. Watering, deepening & laying trench grids in BERWICK & P.S.WITCH.	A.9.A.
	18/7/17		Work as yesterday. Excavating for pipe line at R.E. Dump, METZ. Strengthening roof of RAMC shelter in SHERWOOD AVENUE C.T. Laying trench gates in front line.	A.9.A.
	19/7/17		Work as before. Shoring wall & ceiling of large billet at METZ. Erecting pumping plant at R.E. Dump, METZ, and excavating for & lowering pipe line. Making & erecting camouflaging screens at TRESCHULT & splinter proof shelter for (ADS at Q.21.b.3.b.) Strengthening roof & shelter for RAMC in SHERWOOD AVENUE C.T. (Bn. HQ.) Excavating for one shelter for M.G.C. near top of QUEENS LANE. Fixing trench gates in front line.	A.9.A.

WAR DIARY

INTELLIGENCE SUMMARY

Army Form C. 2118.

511 Field Co R.E.

Place	Date	Hour	Summary of Events and Information	Remarks and references to Appendices
Hop.Pt 59°	25/7/17		Work as yesterday. RE Improvements in the following works:— Deepening + duckboarding TRESCAULT AVENUE C.T. & excavating for revetting shelters; deepening + widening ERITH AVENUE + OLDHAM AVENUE C.T.s; deepening, widening and draining SHERWOOD AVENUE and SHAFTESBURY AVENUE C.T.s; deepening and improving BURNLEY SAP (D"Sap") — (Not more delayed owing to infantry having to stand to with garrison owing to very heavy hostile barrage.) Repairing bottle filling topt as METZ BREWERY. Changing 1"x2" to 4"x4" feet + laying 2 lengths of 4" water main ; fixing Flintson's late casting Murch Gas SUGAR FACTORY, METZ. Reinforcements :— 1.O.R.	f.J.19
	26/7/17		Work as yesterday. Excavating entrance & dugout floor in shelves field in DERBY SUPPORT. Erecting camouflage screen in TRESCAULT AVENUE and covered tanks. Deepening, widening + improving BLACKBURN ALLEY. Moving trestle one stand gate left of BAIRS AVENUE deepening most and ramp + delivering trunk just eft of BAIRS AVENUE. Excavating pit + erecting shelter for M.G.C. left of BAIRS AVENUE.	f.J.19
	27/7/17		Work as yesterday. Deepening, widening + improving OLDHAM ALLEY, BURNLEY ALLEY, deepening + duckboarding TRESCAULT AVENUE, SHERWOOD AVENUE + SHAFTESBURY AVENUE. Erecting shelters in TRESCAULT TRENCH + A.D.S. as Q21.6.3.6. Making + erecting camouflage screen as before.	f.J.19

Army Form C. 2118.

WAR DIARY

INTELLIGENCE SUMMARY

(Erase heading not required.)

5/1 Field Company R.E.

Place	Date	Hour	Summary of Events and Information	Remarks and references to Appendices
Nort Rd 57c	22/7/17		Lowering Tube line at SUGAR FACTORY, METZ, & fixing trough standards, fixing cooling system of fuel tanks, and making engine shed. Testing out cones & at R.E. Dump, METZ.	A.J.18.
	23/7/17		Works as yesterday; deepening widening & improving FRITH AVENUE R.E. supervision and erecting wire entanglements from G.5.a.7.2 to G.5.a.1.3.	A.J.18.
	24/7/17 to 25/7/17 26/7/17		Works as yesterday; deepening, widening & improving BLACKBURN ALLEY. R.E. in conjunction with Brigade Infantry, 174th Brigade sited new Method line 2 Dynnes in front of front line	A.J.18.
	26/7/17		Works as yesterday; erecting barbed wire entanglements in front of STAFFORD TRENCH. (New Outpost line) Also sited 5 strong Points for outpost line.	A.J.18.
	27/7/17		Excavating for 5 Strong Points to outpost line in font of STAFFORD TRENCH, and improving barbed wire entanglements. fixing chevaux-de-frise across road on line of new outpost wire (TRESCAULT RIBÉCOURT RD).	A.J.18.
	28/7/17		Handed over works in line to 63rd Field Coy. R.E. and water supply system to 149 A.T. Coy. R.E. Company cyclists proceeded by road to ABLAINZEVILLE en route for FOSSEUX. 5.0 p.m. Mounted Section moved from EQUANCOURT to ABLAINZEVILLE en route for FOSSEUX	A.J.18.

Army Form C. 2118.

WAR DIARY

INTELLIGENCE SUMMARY

(Erase heading not required.)

511 Field Coy. R.E.

Instructions regarding War Diaries and Intelligence Summaries are contained in F. S. Regs., Part II. and the Staff Manual respectively. Title pages will be prepared in manuscript.

Place	Date	Hour	Summary of Events and Information	Remarks and references to Appendices
Map Ref 51c	28/7/17	7a.m.	Company, with exception of Mounted Section moved from METZ-en-COUTURE by bus to BAPAUME en route for FOSSEUX, entrained at BAPAUME, loaded 174th Inf. Brigade Transport on to train & proceeded by train to SAULTY STATION, detrained. Bde transport at SAULTY, & marched to FOSSEUX (P.16.a.6.8.)	A/18.
FOSSEUX	30/7/17		Improving billets.	A/18.
	31/7/17		Inspection of rifles, equipment, gas helmets, &c. improving billets.	A/18.

J.J. Spencer
Major R.E.
Commdg. 511 Field Coy. R.E.

WAR DIARY or INTELLIGENCE SUMMARY

Army Form C. 2118.

511 Field Coy R.E.

Place	Date	Hour	Summary of Events and Information	Remarks and references to Appendices
Map Ref.	1/8/17		Improving camp. Squad drill, rifle & hill and ricking field classes to D.H.Q.	A 1.8
51º Div AB	2/8/17		Visited D.H.Q. as yesterday. Inspection of gas helmets & lecture on gas. Lecture mask	A 2.8
FOSSEUX	3/8/17		To 4 Section proceeded to MANIN to unload 17st section	A 3.8
	4/8/17		R.E. training. Physical training & squad drill	A 4.8
	5/8/17		Physical training, route march. Work at D.H.Q. on foot	A 5.8
			Rob at D.H.Q. as before. Arranged re D.H.Q.	
			3 O.R. proceeded to Third Army. One O.R. proceeded to 57 Bde to the	
			4/5 R.E. Communication Centre. 1 am and 2 of Section 2 proceeded to BERNEVILLE to	A 6/8
	6/8/17		instruct 174th Brigade in R.E. training	
			70 3 Section proceeded to MANIN to instruct 173rd Inf Bde in R.E. training	A 7.8
			Raising horse standing in FOSSEUX were moved to details	
	7/8/17		3 O.R. proceeded to GR Bde RFA in BOYELLES (T20 a 0.2)(T16 d 1.17) for training	A 7.8
			to Artillery Powers. Brigade Horse Standings at FOSSEUX	
	8/8/17		Brigade training in FOSSEUX. Physical training & details	A 8.8
	9/8/17			A 9.8
	10/8/17		Squad drill. Gas School drill. Physical training & details	A 9.8

Army Form C. 2118.

WAR DIARY
INTELLIGENCE SUMMARY.
(Erase heading not required.)

511 Field Co. R.E.

Instructions regarding War Diaries and Intelligence Summaries are contained in F. S. Regs., Part II. and the Staff Manual respectively. Title pages will be prepared in manuscript.

Place	Date	Hour	Summary of Events and Information	Remarks and references to Appendices
Trop Sep 17 &	11/8/17		Physical training. Infantry & Engineers training for defence and wiring instruction	A.F.1.18
P.b.a.O.2	13/8/17		Physical training. Patrolling.	A.F.1.18.
FOSSEUX	14/8/17		1 New recruit Sapper's from Base.	A.F.1.18
	14/8/17		Physical training, wiring instruction.	
	15/8/17		" + Felling ups + wiring Butts for practice	
	16/8/17			
	16/8/17		2 O.R. proceeded to course at Armoured Car School, AUTEVILLE	A.F.1.18.
	17/8/17		Physical training, cleaning + repairs to wagons, dismantling unwanted camp fittings	
			2 O.R. accidentally wounded	A.F.1.18
			2 L.D. horses sent to M.V.S.	
	18/8/17		Repairing standings to horse troops at D.H.Q. Physical training, wiring, erecting regular	A.F.1.18
			Salvage parties from damaged huts at HERQUELIN.	
	19/8/17		Reserve standings as before. No.1 Section moved to BERNEVILLE to lay road in	A.F.1.18
			Divisional Tactical Exercise	
DUISANS	20/8/17		Coy H.Q. and remaining Section moved from FOSSEUX to No.1 Camp DUISANS. Third Army Rest Camp. Two O.R. admitted to C.C.S.	A.F.1.18

A6945 Wt. W11422/M1160 350,000 12/16 D. D. & L. Forms/C./2118/14.

Army Form C. 2118.

WAR DIARY
INTELLIGENCE SUMMARY

(Erase heading not required.)

511 Field Co RE

Place	Date	Hour	Summary of Events and Information	Remarks and references to Appendices
DUISANS	21/8/17		Sections 1, 2 + 3 took part in Divisional Tactical Exercise in BAILLEULMONT area.	1/8/18
	22/8/17		Sections 1, 2, 3 + 4 Reported Unit at DUISANS	2/9/18
	22/8/17		1 Officer transferred to 504 Field Co R.E.	8/9/18
	22/8/17		1 Officer and 2 O.R. proceeded on advance party to new area; 1 O.R. returned from 291 Bde. R.F.A. at BOSEZLES and 2 O.R. from Chief Gas School HOUTKERQUE.	4/9/18
	22/8/17		Inspection of transport by O.C. + 2nd in command. 1 O.R. admitted C.C.S.	5/9/18
	23/8/17		Inspection of equipment, rifles, gas helmets, kit etc. 3 O.R. admitted to C.C.S.	6/9/18
	24/8/17		5 O.R. admitted to Stationary Hospital. 1 O.R. arrived as reinforcement.	7/9/18
			Preparing for move to new area.	
YPRES AREA	25/8/17	2 a.m.	Company moved by road from DUISANS to ERNY * entrained at ERNY Station & proceeded by rail to G.S.E. 15.70. detrained at GODENAERSVELDTE Station (BELGIUM) & proceeded by road to G.S.E. 15.70.	1/8/18
			Trench Ref. 58.	
	26/8/17		Coy HQ & Sections 1, 2, 3 + 4 move from G.S.E. 15.70 to H.10.a.5.5. (Map 28)	2/9/18
			O.C. inspected forward area to be taken over. met 10 Div.	
	27/8/17	3 a.m.	Digging ditches both sides of road to main ADMIRALS ROAD (Map 28 - G.22.c.7.7) Loading report at IRISH FARM. Ene-Tung Highland Section Artments at Felgo. 118th Division.	7/9/18

WAR DIARY
INTELLIGENCE SUMMARY

511TH FIELD COMPANY, R.E.

Army Form C. 2118.

Place	Date	Hour	Summary of Events and Information	Remarks and references to Appendices
Inf. Rgt. 28	27/9/17		Plelong Track damaged by shell fire & heavy traffic at C.22.d.2.9. Making 20 yards road off hand at divers in at BUFFS ROAD	A/18.
YPRES MEN	28/9/17		N.B. attached Major, 474 Field Co. RE in making overturn a area	B/18.
			One Officer from that Co & L. Bgr attached to Instr. by authority of MA"CDN" 51st Division	
			Three O.R. attached to O.B.E. for work in Girl Workshops.	
	29/9/17		Company HQrs Mounted Station moved to C.25.d.37 (East side of YSER CANAL Bank)	C/18.
			Mounted Section moved to wagon lines at MARSH FARM (H.3.b.3.7.)	
			Took over COMMAND FARM DUMP (WOOD RAILS RR) at 8.15 & H.I. From 474 Fd. Co. RE	
			Reinforcement: 1 O.R.	
			Reconnaissance received for improved front annual shelter g.20 divers in Mac Rac	
	30/9/17		Improvement of dugout accommodation and trenches on East side of CANAL BANK. (C.25.d.0.7)	D/18.
			Preparing road for Tramway forward of OBLONG FARM (C.16.b.4.4) and repairing existing tramway.	
			Reconnoitring for accommodation in Brigade Area.	
			Casualties :— 1 O.R. admitted	
	31/9/17		Works as yesterday	E/18.

J.D. Reynolds
Capt
511 Field Co. R.E.

Army Form C. 2118.

WAR DIARY
INTELLIGENCE SUMMARY
(Erase heading not required.)

511 FIELD COMPANY R.E.

Place	Date	Hour	Summary of Events and Information	Remarks and references to Appendices
Nrth Poperinghe	1/9/17		Improving benches and accommodation. East side of CANAL at C.25.d.3.7. and rearranging for one elephant shelter.	
2nd Shed			Repairing road for tramway at C.20.b.4.4. front of GIBSONS FARM and laying rails.	D.H.
YPRES SALIENT			Repairing existing tramway & relaying part to damaged track.	
			1 O.R. wounded to C.C.S.	
	2/9/17		Works as yesterday. Repairing tramway and preparing cars for siding at C.15.d.4.1. also side of Light Railway (near CANADIAN FARM) Switching also Shelter at C.25.d.2.5.	R.H.L.
	3/9/17		Works as yesterday	R.H.L.
			1 O.R. wounded in action	
	4/9/17		Excavating occupied dugout floor in hy shell pits at C.25.d.9.7. Dismantling huts 1 & 2 & Repairing ft & erecting 2 elephant shelters. Repairing ft & erecting new shelter at C.25.d.4.2. Laying concrete emplacement & erecting & shelter for 174th Bde. Laying in track at C.15.f.8.8. (GATWICK COTTAGE) to provide shelter. Repairing damaged tramway at C.15 f.6.4. Preparing roadway for & laying tramway.	R.H.L.
	5/9/17		Works as yesterday. Laying rails at C.13. F.2.5. to provide shelter.	W.H.L.
	6/9/17		R.E. Supervision of following works :- Laying and wiring shelter over trenches in Old German line from C.16.f.80.18 to C.16.c.60.50. Wiring, drawing & repairing shelter.	W.H.L.

WAR DIARY

INTELLIGENCE SUMMARY — 511 Field Coy R.E.

Army Form C. 2118.

(2)

Place	Date	Hour	Summary of Events and Information	Remarks and references to Appendices
Thos Rd Sheet 28 YPRES Salient	6/9/17		Trs 185 & 191 and Trs 171, 172 and 175 in CANOE TRENCH	A.W.L.
	7/9/17		R.E. Supervision of Infantry on the following works:— Excavating for & fixing large English steel shelters at C.25.d.3,7. and re-inforcing concrete covering etc. Erecting 16 shelters for 174 Bde H.Q. staff. Erecting 14 shelters to TMP at C.17 c.16. Altering MEBU No.130 at C.17 c.1.7. + preparing site for erection of shelter. Altering MEBUS Nos 188 to 192 (C.16.d.2.6 to C.10 d.1.6.). Pumping out and clearing shelter Nos 173 to 182 (C.16.b.6.9.7). Making additional 12 ft accommodation at KULTUR FARM (C.16.c.5D.60) 1.O.R. evacuated sick.	A.W.L.
	8/9/17		Erecting shelters as yesterday. Chimney repairs and constructing hindh in M.A. German line at C.16 c.6.5. to provide 25 ft accommodation. R.E. Supervision of Infantry on following works:— Erecting four small English shelters at MEBU No.120. (C.17 c.1.7.) and three shelters at C.17 c.16. Altering and raising CARAMEL TRENCH (C.16.6. central), repairing damaged portions + being established. Reinforcements:— 1.O.R.	A.W.L.
	9/9/17		NURSE TMM (C.22.b.5.3):— Preparing foundation of structure in CANE TRENCH. Erecting four English MEBUs at MEBUS at C.17 C.17. Pumping out sheets + clearing shelter Nos 171 to 182	A.W.L.

WAR DIARY
INTELLIGENCE SUMMARY

Army Form C. 2118.

5/1 Field Co. R.E.

Place	Date	Hour	Summary of Events and Information	Remarks and references to Appendices
Trip Ref 28 YPRES	9/9/17		at C.16.b.1.97 and shelters Too 184 to 194 C.10.d.2.5 & C.10.d.4.5. Making trench lattice where possible. When work at 14.c Attwinder's 1 Pt. Officer	15 N.1
	10/9/17		Reinforcements. 1.O.R. Ref Inspection on the following works. Repairing duckboarding, improving existing accommodation Enemy are now English shelters at RAMC Relief Bay (C.17.c.12.15) and building + sandbagging in shelters Enemy aire's. laying track. Pumping out MEBs. 70. 170 at C.17.c.17. + sandbagging + duckboarding shelters Pumping + clearing MEBs. No. 183 & 194 draining, clearing and laying duckboards in shelters at HUSER HOLLOW (C.11.d.1.2) & HUSER HOLLOW (C.11.d.4.0). Erecting English steel shelters at 174 Bde HQ as before. Supervising transportation of material English shelters from GARDE TRETON to MED do HIBOU (C.7.a.a.b)	15 M.1
			2.O.R. encounted sick	
	11/9/17		Works as yesterday 1.O.R. encounted sick	10. M.2
	12/9/17		Works as yesterday. Removed tres/poraner shelters with MEBs. Nos 175 and subsequent tramlines for additional shelters Pumping out + clearing MEBs Nos. 115 & 184 + 170. 4783 in extension TRENCH	15 M.L

WAR DIARY
INTELLIGENCE SUMMARY. 571 Field C.R.E.

Army Form C. 2118.

Place	Date	Hour	Summary of Events and Information	Remarks and references to Appendices
Trip Ref 28. Ypres Salient	12/9/17		Erecting 4 small English Shelters East of STEENBEEK. Casualties: Failed 2 O.R. Wounded 3 O.R. (one Serb)	15 M.R.
	13/9/17		Works on yesterday. Engineers meeting in O.C. Mess. (O.S.M.R. CAPTURE meeting. Striking 2 large English Shelters H.17.h.B66. Cart-diggers continue demolition shelter at C.10.d central & carrying out cleaning work. RE supervision on filling roads. Making dugouts at Hailebrite wood.	15 M.R.
	14/9/17		Of 100 yours on OB Trench 16.b.2.52.55 & C.6.c.60w). Carrying 100m NEBU to 120. Improving drainage around MEBU. Erecting 1 small English Shelter near at C.17.c.a.7 & one at 26.6.32.33. Starting up trench to 2 large dugouts at C.25 al.37.	15 M.R.
			Slaapy and debris & repairing dugouts at C.25 cl.37 dugouts as shell fire.	
			Casualties 2 O.R. Casualties 5 O.R. (sich) Wounded – Not on duty.	
	15/9/17		Shoring side Meeting 18 shelter Heritage Wood and clean in CHEMO Track #6.5 a.127. Erecting new shelter at rear of MEBU 120, tearing down 1400 & carrying dumps. Erecting too English Shelter in Lyvallon. Moving hit dumps dumps to lives. To various scholar turbines at C.B.C.76. Improving & capital shelters in C.B.C.	15 M.R.

Army Form C. 2118.

WAR DIARY
INTELLIGENCE SUMMARY
(Erase heading not required.)

Place	Date	Hour	Summary of Events and Information	Remarks and references to Appendices
Trench Raid 28 YPRES Salient	16/9/17		Firing Welshes in CALIFORNIA TRENCH and Sprinkler shelter as yesterday. MH Raid No. 20	
			Yesterday. Pumping out Trenches at C.21.6.4.0. (HYPER HOLLOW) & Laying duckwalk.	W.N.1
			Also Pumping out and cleaning MEBU No. 21.9.a. C.21.a.7.5. (HYPER WALK). MEBU was incorporating	
	17/9/17		Firing welshes in CALIFORNIA TRENCH. Clearing MEBUs for OTHER TRENCH shelter.	
			Carrying two Pigeon fountains to buzz on STEENBEEK at C.5.d.10. and	W.N.1
			anything working. Clearing Rees at VANCOUVER (C.6.c.8.5. & C.6.a.15.0. Digging Cables	
			& Front to 17a.M. Sto. Battle Maps.	
			Casualties: 1.O.R. wounded. 1 O.R. evacuated to P.C.M. sick	
	18/9/17		Firing welshes in CALIFORNIA TRENCH entry OP on CATHOPS TRENCH at C.21.9.5.	
			Burying & cleaning rees of entrance to MEBU No. 120. Clearing out & laying concrete	W.N.1
			shelter on CROSS TRENCH. Clearing piles on TRIANGLE (C.21.16 and C.21.15.0)	
			Pigeon new bridge on STEENBEEK. Making new water fitting near dressing.	
			Casualties: 1 O.R. wounded. 3 O.R. evacuated P.C.M. sick.	
	19/9/17		2 killed and 5 horses wounded by shell fire	
			Erecting 18 shelters & preparing storage hutch & drains in CALIFORNIA TRENCH (C.22.6.7.0)	
			1.O.R. admits hospital	

WAR DIARY
INTELLIGENCE SUMMARY

Army Form C. 2118.

511 Field Co. R.E.

Place	Date	Hour	Summary of Events and Information	Remarks and references to Appendices
Map Ref. 28 N.W.	28/9/17	2.0 a.m	Sections paraded at 2.0 a.m. to take part in offensive operations with 174th Infantry Brigade, in conjunction with a Brigade of 57th Division on the left and the 173rd Infantry Brigade (58th Division) on the right.	L.P.S
YPRES SALIENT			Sections 1 and 2 proceeded to GATWICK COTTAGE (C.15.d.8.6.), and advanced bay by bay with Sections 3 and 4 proceeded to KULTUR FARM (CANADIAN RESERVE) at C.15.c.7.8.	
	{Sept 29 29/9/17 and 21/9/17}		Consolidating the shell holes taken with sandbags, revetment at BENOM (D.1.a 35.25.) Constructing shell slab shelter in use mis. post with less ammunition and making new pin point mit. post	H.R
			Reconnaissance at D.I.G. 2.0. Supervision of parties on carrying up trench mats + R.E. tools from forward dump at C.12. a.33. to D.7. a.58. Parts around shelter made in used to mine shaft to form canal bank dump 3 to Zwarch dump.	
	21/9/17		Casualties:- Killed:- 1 O.R. Wounded:- 6. O.R. Evacuated sick. 1 O.T. 1 Army horse evacuated to mobile Veterinary section. Reinforcements:- 9. O.R.	
	{Sept 4 24/9/17 26 Sept 1917}		Excavating + preparing to erect a base small English steel shelters at CLUSTER HOUSE (C.7.A.5.8) Excavating for two small English steel shelters, clearing away rust at entrance + starting up entrance of MEBU at HUBNER FARM (D.1. C.45. 65)	L.O.R

WAR DIARY
INTELLIGENCE SUMMARY

(Erase heading not required.)

5/1 Field, R.E.

Army Form C. 2118.

Place	Date	Hour	Summary of Events and Information	Remarks and references to Appendices
YPRES SALIENT	Sept/Oct 28 21/9/17 and 22/9/17	Night	Carrying material from ST JULIEN to erecting small steel English Shelters at CLUSTER HOUSES and WURST FARM	
	Night		do do do Gateway — Forecast of for our small English shelters erectings	
	22nd/23rd Sept 1917	Night	Sandbag wall 21 Company Hqrs as protection against shrapnel. Improving material at ADAMS FARM for erection of Shelter at HUBNER FARM	
	23/9/17		Casualties:- 1 O.R. wounded. R.O.R. sent to hospital sick. 3 O.R. evacuated to C.C.S. sick.	
	Sept/Oct 23/24 and Sept 1917	Night	Erecting small English shelters and observation Post of R.E. CLUSTER HOUSES (D.I.2.37.D.2.)	
			Casualties:- 1 O.R. evacuated sick to C.C.S. Reinforcements:- 3 O.R.	
		Night	Erecting small English shelters at CLUSTER HOUSES.	
	24/25/9/17 25/9/17	Sept 1917	Sections 1 and 2 moved from GATWICK COTTAGE to YSER work Bank. Erecting Observation Post at D.7.A.3.1 Section 3 moved from CANAL BANK to PESEL HOEK.	

WAR DIARY / INTELLIGENCE SUMMARY

Army Form C. 2118.

511 Field Co. R.E.

(8)

Instructions regarding War Diaries and Intelligence Summaries are contained in F.S. Regs., Part II, and the Staff Manual respectively. Title pages will be prepared in manuscript.

Place	Date	Hour	Summary of Events and Information	Remarks and references to Appendices
Trop. Pol. 28.	25/9/17		Casualties:- Killed:- 1.O.R. Wounded:- 4. O.R.	
YPRES SALIENT			1. O.R. evacuated sick.	
	26/9/17		Hdqrs., Nos. 1 and 2 Sections moved from CHITRAL BARN to HUZZA BARN at MARSH HILL	
			FARM (H.3.B.37) Nos. 3 & 4 Sections moved from KULTUR FARM to MARSHES FARM.	
			Advance party proceeded to new area.	
	27/9/17	2.30 p.m.	Nos. 2, 3 & 4 Sections left MARSHES FARM at 2.30 p.m. and proceeded to PESELHOEK	
			Station. Entire Brigade transport and entrained at 7.30 p.m. to proceed to new area.	
		7 p.m.	Remainder Section moved from MARSHES FARM by rail to SAUGHEN	
HAZEBROUCK 5A	28/9/17	2.30 a.m.	Company less Remainder Section detained at PIEMEN & entrained to Brigade Transport	
and CALAIS 13			rested until 8.30 a.m. & proceeded by road to SAUGHEN.	
			Sections 3 & 4 arrived at BONNINGUES 1 + Coy H.Q. Sections 1 and 2 arrived MAZORI	
			lines at SAUGHEN.	
	29/9/17		Company resting.	
	30/9/17	9.00 a.m.	Inspection of Equipment 1 + Feb. required week	
			1 Officer proceeded to R.M. Army School, TOTTENGHEM + 1 Officer to VIII Corps Gas School	
			Sections 3 & 4 constructing ranges at GUEMY and ANDLETHUN	

Commd. 511 Field Co. R.E.

WAR DIARY
INTELLIGENCE SUMMARY
(Erase heading not required.)

Army Form C. 2118.

Vol 10

511TH FIELD COMPANY, R.E.

Place	Date	Hour	Summary of Events and Information	Remarks and references to Appendices
CALAIS 13.F.3. SPYCKER	1/10/17		Squad drill for No. 2, 3.0 + Mounted Section	
			Nos. 3 & 4 Sections:- Constructing Tunnel & Nor barge near FORET D'EPERLEQUE (on WATTEN ROAD) and excavating & gravel & carrying same to billets	J.R.
	2/10/17		Lining tombs at LAFERME DE LA MOTTE, and making overhead cover to ranges at GUEMY. Reveting Range trench and making overhead cover to ranges at GUEMY.	
			Works as yesterday to Tunnels & Nor barge and repairs & improvements to billets at ARDREHEM and BOURNINGHEM. Constructing Rifle Range at GUEMY.	F.J.B.
	3/10/17		Works as yesterday Evening Bugece lates at LIQUES.	J.R.
	4/10/17		2 O.R. evacuated sick to hospital	
	5/10/17		1 O.R. attached to XVIII Corps Topographical Section, to duty. Works as yesterday	F.J.B.
	6/10/17		2 O.R. admitted hospital	
	7/10/17		Works as before	F.J.B.
	8/10/17		3 O.R. proceeded to Fifth Army Rest Camp	
	9/10/17	1 p.m.	Mounted Section and Cyclists proceeded to new area & commenced to the right of ETRUSTEM	J.R.
			4 L.D. horses arrived	

WAR DIARY
INTELLIGENCE SUMMARY
(Erase heading not required.)

Army Form C. 2118.

511TH FIELD COMPANY, R.E.

Place	Date	Hour	Summary of Events and Information	Remarks and references to Appendices
SAMETTEN	9/10/17	9.0 a.m.	Company less mounted section and cyclists, marched by road to LICQUES and proceeded by Motor lorry to HOSPITAL FARM CAMP (Map 28 NW. B.10.d.2.2.) Transport moved from ERINGHEM and joined Unit at HOSPITAL FARM CAMP.	J.R.
Map 28 NW.	10/10/17		Collecting material for and erecting NISSEN BOW HUTS at HOSPITAL FARM CAMP. Improving camp, making Rose lines. Reconnoitring site and roads to be done at GHENT COTTAGES (B.22.d.7.0.) and at New Camp at B.21.d.7.5.	J.R.
	11/10/17		Work at HOSPITAL FARM CAMP as yesterday. Building road, partly of corduroy and partly of expanded metal, round horse standings at GHENT COTTAGES. Carrying materials for erecting NISSEN Bow huts & completing huts in course of erection at SIEGE CAMP (B.21.d.7.5. South of PIONEER FARM) 2. O.R. admitted hospital sick. 1. O.R. returned from hospital. 2. O.R. rejoined sick.	J.R.
	12/10/17		Work at HOSPITAL FARM CAMP and GHENT FARM as before. Erecting NISSEN Bow huts at Camp at A.30.d.9.7. Skinny and at FANTASIO FARM CAMP at B.21.d.7.5. Erecting Nissen huts at various camps as above. Latter. Erecting horse standings at C.25.a.4.4. (near ESSEX FARM).	J.R.
	13/10/17		Erecting Nissen huts at camp at A.2+a.5.3. 1. O.R. admitted hospital sick.	J.R.

WAR DIARY

INTELLIGENCE SUMMARY

Army Form C. 2118.

511TH FIELD COMPANY, R.E.

(3)

Place	Date	Hour	Summary of Events and Information	Remarks and references to Appendices
Rop Rd.28.M.14/1017	14/10/17		Works as yesterday. Erecting Nissen huts at FANTASIO FARM (Camp No 3) at J.3.1.d.9.5.	7918
	15/10/17		do do Building spinter-proof wall round force station + levelling sand	4/R
			with expanded metal at No 3. Brick Stables (B.22. d. 65.10.)	4/R
	16/10/17		3 Reinforcements reported (temporarily attached to 503 Fld Coy R.E.)	
	17/10/17		do	4/R
	17/10/17		1. O.R. Evacuated sick.	
	18/10/17 to 20/10/17		Works as before.	7/R
	21/10/17		Works as before. Erecting 10 NISSEN HUTS at LA FLAURE, POPERINGHE (Trps 28.inn G.2.d.9.3.)	1.1.R
			1 Officer and 12. O.R. proceeded to 174th Inf Bde to set out Training Ground at L.8.d.9.2 Trps	
			23/27	
	22/10/17		Works as yesterday.	8918
			Reinforcements:- 23. O.R.	
			1 O.R. discharged from hospital	
	23/10/17		Works as before.	918
			1 Officer + 12 O.R. of this Unit attached to 174 Bde returned to duty.	

WAR DIARY

~~INTELLIGENCE SUMMARY~~

Army Form C. 2118.

511TH FIELD COMPANY, R.E.

Place	Date	Hour	Summary of Events and Information	Remarks and references to Appendices
Map Ref. L 28 IW	24/7/17		Preparation for move. Four O.R. (carpenters) attached R.E. Store for duty	A.19.R
	25/7/17		Dismounted portion of Company moved from HOSPITAL FARM CAMP (B.19.d.2.2.) to YSER CANAL BANK (C.25.a.5.5)	A.19
			1 Officer + 10 O.R. of Divisional Observers attached for same duties	
			1 Officer + 50 O.R. attached for duty stations from 176th Inf. Bde.	
			1 O.R. attached for duty at Fort Mobility	
	26/7/17		Enemy taking up accommodation in CANE TRENCH (reg. sec.) in Piebarmon	
			Co. and way forward to GLOSTER FARM (V.19.b.3.3) transferring trenches in 12 hour	
			10 m.g. L.R. HURST PARK (20 C.3.7) between the Bank side Canal line C.25.a.7.5	
			L25 d. 95.75 during the night – timber at C.25 a. 5.5	
			Spare party of 4th Div. side – MULE HEAD – C.25.a.1.1. 12 m.g. 40m light rlys	
			from Inf. school 1.5m telephone lines etc. C.25 a.2 to SP rd. forward through	
			the border of Basin of YPERLEE	
			Casualties — 3 O.R. wounded	
			Attached Major Ince moved to No. 3 BETHLEHEM FARM	£1.19

WAR DIARY
INTELLIGENCE SUMMARY
(Erase heading not required.)

Army Form C. 2118.

517TH FIELD COMPANY, R.E.

Place	Date	Hour	Summary of Events and Information	Remarks and references to Appendices
Trap Rd. 28.N.M	27/10/17		Works as yesterday. Continuing Metalled Road from TYRES-BOESINGHE ROAD (C.19.c.2.2.) to D.H.Q. Erecting Elephants C.25.R. and spendifores at same. B.22.a.7.1. Repairing Duckwalk past Hurst Park — Hurst Park. Casualties 2 O.R. wounded. 1 O.R. (MILNER) missing. Punctures nil. B. 1 O.R. Wounded Listou moved from HOSPITAL FARM CAMP (B.20.d.1.2) to POTIZHAEK (A.26. & B.7.)	1078
	28/10/17		Works as yesterday. Repairing the roads of Base Road nebuilt at C.17. & C.19 as L.M.me.	1078
	29/10/17		Works as yesterday. Erecting Nissan Hutsat C.19.c.s.1. Casualties. Killed. 2.O.R. Wounded. 1 O.R. and 1 O.R attacks.	1078
	30/10/17		Works as yesterday. 1 Officer and 1 O.R. returned from XVIII Corps. S. School.	1078
	31/10/17		Works as yesterday.	1078

F.N. Rycroft Major R.E.
Commd. 517 Field Coy.

WAR DIARY

INTELLIGENCE SUMMARY

(Erase heading not required.)

Army Form C. 2118.

5111TH FIELD COMPANY, R.E.

Place	Date	Hour	Summary of Events and Information	Remarks and references to Appendices
Map 28 NW	1/11/17		Repair + maintenance of Southern Duckboard Track - HURST PARK to GLOSTER	
YPRES			FARM. Erecting large elephant shelter at C.25.a.5.5. for RAMC and	
SALIENT			repairing shelters + dugouts at C.25.a.5.5. Preparing camp as CAVE	A.19
			POST (C.9 central), erecting shelters	
			1. O.R. evacuated sick	
	2/11/17		1. O.R. returned to Unit from XVIII Corps Rfps. section.	F.19
	3/11/17		Works as yesterday.	
			No. 4 Section moved from CANAL BANK (C.25.A.5.5.) to CADE POST CAMP (C.9 central)	H.19
	4/11/17 to 6/11/17		Works as yesterday	
			1. O.R. (attached R Reinforced) 1. O.R. admitted Hospital sick, 1.O.R. returned to Unit Hospital sick	A.19
			Works as yesterday	
	5/11/17		Casualties:- 1.O.R. wounded. 1.O.R. (A. Hackes) Killed	A.19
	6/11/17		Attached - 3 Officers 37.O.R. 9/17th Bde. 7 M.3. attached for duty as Pioneers	A.19
			Detached - 1 Officer + O.R. attached from 17th Bde. returned to respective Batns.	

WAR DIARY
INTELLIGENCE SUMMARY
(Erase heading not required.)

Army Form C. 2118.

511TH FIELD COMPANY, R.E.

Place	Date	Hour	Summary of Events and Information	Remarks and references to Appendices
Map 28 NW	7/11/17		Works as yesterday. Sandbagging Shelters at No. 2 BRIELEN Stables (B.22.d.7.1.)	J.J.S.
	8/11/17		1 Officer & 1 O.R. returned from course at Fifth Army School, TOUTENCOURT. Works as before	J.J.S.
	9/11/17		3 O.R. admitted hospital (sick)	J.J.S.
	10/11/17		Works as yesterday; improving entrance to and interior of GLOSTER FARM. Works as before	J.J.S.
	11/11/17		No. 4 Section moved from CANE POST CAMP (C.9. central) to CANAL BANK (C.25.a.5.5.) No. 3 d⁰ from CANAL BANK (C.25.a.5.5.) to CANE POST CAMP (C.9. central)	J.J.S.
	12/11/17 to 14/11/17		Works as yesterday. 1 Officer & 2 O.R. proceeded to Fifth Army Infantry School TOUTENCOURT, for course. Works as yesterday; preparing site for stabling at TURCO FARM.	J.J.S.
	15/11/17		HdQrs, Sections 1, 3 & 4 moved from CANAL BANK (Map 28 NW. C.25.a.5.5.) to PORTSDOWN CAMP (X.25. a.4.1. Sheet 19 S.E.) Section 3 moved from CANE POST CAMP (C.9. central, Sheet 28 NW) to d⁰	J.J.S.

Army Form C. 2118.

(3)

WAR DIARY

INTELLIGENCE SUMMARY

(Erase heading not required.)

511 Field Coy. R.E.

Place	Date	Hour	Summary of Events and Information	Remarks and references to Appendices
	15/10/17		Mounted Section moved from PESELHOEK (A.21.a.8.7 Sheet 28 NW) to do.	22.R.S.
Trap 28 J.19 S.E.	16/10/17		Company billets at PORTSDOWN CAMP, PROVEN, and providing additional accommodation	22.S.
PROVEN AREA	17/10/17		Erecting "Nissen" huts at PORTSMOUTH CAMP (178th Bde Hdqrs) at N.30.d.05.35.	99.R.
			Infantry training of recent reinforcements	
	19/10/17		Erecting huts as yesterday. Instructions received for Company to proceed to BRIELEN (B.30.C.2.8) to work on Forward Roads under C.E., II Corps	H.
			1 Officer + 25 O.R. proceeded to XIX Corps Workshops at ONDANK (Sheet 28, A.5.C.4.7.) for duty.	
	19/10/17		Erecting huts in adjacent camps. Infantry training of recent reinforcements. Advance party moved from ONDANK and took over camp from a Field Coy of 5th Divn.	22.R.
Trap. 28 N.W.			at Trap 28. B.30.C.2.8.	
YPRES Area	20/10/17		Preparing for move. Work in camps in PROVEN AREA handed over to 504 Field C. R.E.	19.R.
	21/10/17		Company moved from PORTSDOWN CAMP to camp at sheet 28, B.30.C.2.8.	22.S.
			1 Officer + 25 O.R at ONDANK repairs. Carrying at new camp	
	22/10/17		Improving camp and horse lines. Continued	22.R.

WAR DIARY
INTELLIGENCE SUMMARY.

Army Form C. 2118.

511 Field Coy R.E.

Place	Date	Hour	Summary of Events and Information	Remarks and references to Appendices
Ypres	28.11.17 23/11/17		Improving billets & horse lines	
	24/11/17		Reform road formation to Battery positions at ST JULIEN - LANGEMARCK ROAD (U.29.d.60.20. to U.29.d.90.35.) Erecting single sheet & pick steel shelter for 108th Battery at SNIPER HOUSE (U.29.d.7.2.); preparing site for large Trench steel shelter for 174th Battery at BIRD HOUSE (U.29.d.6.8.) and construction of approach road for 112th Battery & Artillery at C.6.a.6.9. and for 5th Siege Battery at C.6.a.3.2. 4 O.R. admitted to field amb.	L.R.
	25/11/17		Construction of approach roads to gun positions at 309th Battery on the ST JULIEN - LANGEMARCK ROAD (U.29.d.6.1. to U.29.d.90.35.), Sandbagging shelter for 108th Battery at SNIPER HOUSE (U.29.d.7.5.), and erecting sandbag wall round gun emplacement (U.29.d.6.6.). Sawing shellpile & constructing road to gun emplacement at U.29.d.1.5.4. for 111 Siege Battery. Construction of approach roads for heavy artillery at C.6.a.3.2.(5th Siege Battery position) 1 O.R. evacuated (sick) 4 O.R. admitted hospital (sick)	J.R.
			Continued	

WAR DIARY / INTELLIGENCE SUMMARY

Army Form C. 2118.

511 FIELD COY R.E.

Place	Date	Hour	Summary of Events and Information	Remarks and references to Appendices
Mob.Rd.	26/11/17		Preparing road formation to 65th Group A.U. on ST JULIEN - LANGEMARCK ROAD (U.29.d.4.4 to U.29.d.7.7). Construction of new approaches to gun emplacements of 11st Siege Battery (65th Group) at U.29.d.66. Erecting sandbag wall round new gun emplacements & for 108th Battery (46th Group); construction of approach roads for 174th and 108th Batteries (46th Group) at C.6.a.8.2.	
28.11.17			Award of Military Cross to 2nd Lieut F.P. HUGHES R.E.(T) (Ref. 58th Div R.O. 835 of 29/11/17)	A.J.B.
	27/11/17		Works as yesterday.	
			2 O.R. admitted to hospital (sick) 1 O.R. evacuated (sick)	J.O.S.
		3.50p.m.	Advance party proceeded from Boesinghe to Proven to entrain for HAZEBROUCK area (Lieut MAZ BROWN & 5.12 O.Rs. - Grouse 5th)	
			Rear Area by HATRE (Lieut MAX BROWN & 5.12 O.Rs. - Grouse 5th)	
Mob. HAZEBROUCK	28/11/17	9.00am	Advance party arrived by train & proceeded to Billets	J.J.H.
S.H.		11.08am	Mounted section moved to ST OMER-STEENBECQUE en route for same area.	
			Preparing for move & cleaning up in billets. 1 O.R. evacuated (sick)	
			4 O.R. discharged hospital	
			Work on 2nd horse area tended over to 179th Tunnelling Coy R.E.	
	10.35 p.m.		Orders received from 2nd Cavalry Div (G.924 of 27/11/17) that Company not to move —	

Army Form C. 2118.

WAR DIARY
INTELLIGENCE SUMMARY.
(Erase heading not required.)

511th FIELD COMPANY R.E.

Place	Date	Hour	Summary of Events and Information	Remarks and references to Appendices
CALAIS	28/11/17		Proceed to BAINGHEM (Lastres Map 2 C)	
MAP 13	29/11/17	9.20 am	Company proceeded by lorries to BAINGHEM. Lorries were first to be held with Belgian troops. Proceeded by to LANDRETHUN-LE-NORD and found billets in	H.S.
			Snowy freeze	
			Company to work	
	30/11/17		Instructions received from CRE 5th Division to proceed to BAINGHEM-LE-COMTE (CALAIS 13, Square 3E).	H.S.
		3.0pm	Company proceeded by march route to BAINGHEM-LE-COMTE (CALAIS 13, Square 3E)	

J H Howarth
Major R.E.
Comm'd'g 511th Field Co R.E.

WAR DIARY

INTELLIGENCE SUMMARY

Volume 11

511TH FIELD COMPANY, R.E.

Army Form C. 2118.

Place	Date	Hour	Summary of Events and Information	Remarks and references to Appendices
CALAIS N.H.D.13 BONNINGHEM 22. C.27.2.4.	1/4/17		Improving billets.	WAR
	2/4/17		Company well + improving billets. Transport arrived.	WAR
	3/4/17		Company well, Company drill, Kit inspection. Route march, Company drill, Kit inspection.	WAR
		10.0	Proceeded to service in the Shed WELLES- LES-Bâgum.	WAR
	4/4/17		Company drill, overhauling + repairing vehicles.	WAR
	5/4/17		" " Preparations for move.	WAR
LUMBRES	6/4/17	8.30 a.m.	Company proceeded from BONNINGHEM-COMTE to SAMETTE CAMP LUMBRES by march route.	WAR
		12 pm	Ser Reserves arrived.	
	7/4/17	6.30 am	Inspected Section and transport preceded by road to new area.	WAR
	8/4/17	5 am	Company less transport later road to WIZERNES by road, + moved to VLAMERTINGHE + Proceeded by march route to "B" Lines R.I.S.K.S.L. (sheet 28 N.W.)	WAR
VLAMERTINGHE	9/4/17		Advance Party of 1 Officer + 4 N.C.O. proceeded to arrange accommodation for Company + take over work from 205 Field Co. R.E.	WAR

Army Form C. 2118.

WAR DIARY
INTELLIGENCE SUMMARY.
(Erase heading not required.)

511TH FIELD COMPANY, R.E.

Place	Date	Hour	Summary of Events and Information	Remarks and references to Appendices
Prob Q. 22 MM	9/12/17		Company arrived at "D" Camp from LUMBRES.	AJK
	10/12/17		Dismounted portion of Company march from "D" Camp PROVEN to dugouts on East Bank YSER CANAL Park at C.13.c.3.6.	AJK
	11/12/17		2 Reinforcements arrived. 2 O.R. evacuated.	AJK
			Maintenance of duckboard track "A" and LANGEMARCK Road Back + dubbing New Mule Trail SCHAETZBOOM. Pigeoness and dining huts for SCHAETZBOOM, Wet Houses, Maintenance of incident track "B" constructing northern approach to bridge over STEENBEEK at U.28.c.9.7. Repairing + improving approach to central CANAL BANK	AJK
			Maintenance Mule duckboard track "A" + "B" and LANGEMARCK ROAD track, dubbing LANGEMARCK track. Repairing trip to No. MOTOR wire bridge over STEENBEEK at U.28.c.9.7 which had been destroyed by shellfire, and constructing northern approach to this bridge. Repairing + improving huts in camp at CANAL BANK and improving existing + erecting structural huts at these camps (D.30.a.8.2)	AJK

continued

WAR DIARY
INTELLIGENCE SUMMARY.
(Erase heading not required.)

Army Form C. 2118.

511TH FIELD COMPANY, R.E.

Place	Date	Hour	Summary of Events and Information	Remarks and references to Appendices
Feb 28 M.M.	13/4/17		Works as yesterday. Enemy shelled 144 M Rd & Moss	
			Lavenborg & gun pits. 4 Siding additional to pork of string holes, Compromis Farm.	
			WATER HOUSES, SENEGAL FARM AND TRIBE FARM.	
		14/4/17	4 Officers 108 O.R. of 17th M Konl Bn attached for duty and rations, as from 13th instant, as Shipping Company.	131/-
			I.O.R. accidentally wounded by rifle S.A.A. — not sure duty.	
		15/4/17	Improving accommodation at EAGLE TRENCH (U.23.A.61 & U.23.A.69). This work was transferred to Army Library. Other works as yesterday.	132/-
		16/4/17	Works as yesterday.	
			I.O.R. admitted hospital (sick)	
		17/4/17	Works on EAGLE TRENCH as before. Reinforcing & sheltered tracks. A.S.B. & marking out in advance of LANGEMARCK FORD TRACK, and laying track for IMBROS HOUSE & OLGA HOUSES. Improving accommodation in camp & stables. Reconnoitring for and sitting out CORPS LINE from U.17.a.1.1. to U.24.c.1.1. Works as detailed until no before.	132/-
			I.O.R. admitted hospital (sick)	144/-

Army Form C. 2118.

WAR DIARY
of
INTELLIGENCE SUMMARY.
(Erase heading not required.)

Instructions regarding War Diaries and Intelligence Summaries are contained in F. S. Regs., Part II. and the Staff Manual respectively. Title pages will be prepared in manuscript.

Place	Date	Hour	Summary of Events and Information	Remarks and references to Appendices
Trap. 28 NW 17/23			Not left. Relaying LANGEMARCK – SCHREIBOOM ROAD from U.23.2.10.40. to	
	18/2/17		U.23.1.20.30	W.R.E.
			Works as yesterday	
			2 O.R. admitted sick. 1 O.R. admitted hospital (sick)	
			1 Officer 1 O.R. returned from duties at Loth Army Infantry L.M.G. TOURNEHEM.	W.R.E.
	19/2/17		Works as yesterday.	
			Reinforcements 5. O.R.	
			LANGEMARCK	
			Court of Enquiry ordered by CRE 5th Division was held to investigate circumstances	
			of the accidental wounding of 1 O.R. (Sapper WELHAM D. No 559039) on 13/2/17	
			on which date this man was (the first man wounded to our day)	I.S.H.
	20/2/17		Works as yesterday. Erecting shelters at U.23.4 bit A. Broaning station.	
			INKERMAN EAGLE - BEAR and WHITE TRENCHES. Searching two lean-tos	
			emplacements at TRUBE HOSPITAL	
			Conclusions of Court of Enquiry is accepted regarding of Sapper WELHAM D.559039	W.R.E.
	21/2/17		Resuming two lean-tos emplacements at TRUBE FARM HOSPITAL + digging pit	
			at MEBUS near it + constructing two bunkers (Tasks handed over to Infantry F.C.)	W.R.E.

WAR DIARY or INTELLIGENCE SUMMARY

(Erase heading not required.)

Army Form C. 2118.

Instructions regarding War Diaries and Intelligence Summaries are contained in F. S. Regs., Part II. and the Staff Manual respectively. Title pages will be prepared in manuscript.

611th FIELD COMPANY R.E.

Place	Date	Hour	Summary of Events and Information	Remarks and references to Appendices
Map 28 NW	21/7/17		Gassing for works at SIEGEL FARM & WATER HOUSES. Repairing loop defences at U.7.d.31, M.23.b.32, M.24.a.59, M.24.c.12. Maintenance of "B" track, & laying mat (duck) from LANGEMARCK R.R. track to TAUBE FARM.	
			1 O.R. admitted hospital (sick).	J.W.K.
	22/7/17		Work to ENGELL, WHITE and BATH TRENCHES as before. Work to front line setting out & driving new entanglement from U.30.a.30 to U.17.a.25. Laying new duck completements & setting out line of new front TAUBE FARM to SIEGEL FARM. Restoration of infantry railway and RE sidings at EAGLE & CONDÉ HOUSE DUMPS. Carrying mule tracks EAGLE DUMP to FERDINAN HOUSE and BREWERY. Repairs / maintenance of "A" "B" and LANGEMARCK ROAD TRACKS & roadway duckboard track LANGEMARCK ROAD TRACK to TAUBE FARM. North of SENEGAL FARM and WATER HOUSES by REME. Ewing Stores at 17m.R.29. Huge Hayes enemies' marks to Cumbrai B.30.a.93. Three Horse lines move from "P" camp, PESELHOEK, to B.20.R.92. 1 O.R. reverted to duty.	W.K.

WAR DIARY
or
INTELLIGENCE SUMMARY.
(Erase heading not required.)

Army Form C. 2118.

Instructions regarding War Diaries and Intelligence Summaries are contained in F.S. Regs., Part II. and the Staff Manual respectively. Title pages will be prepared in manuscript.

Place	Date	Hour	Summary of Events and Information	Remarks and references to Appendices
Map 28 (BELGIUM)	23/12/17		1 O.R. twice stuck (sick)	WD1
	24/12/17		Casualties: 1 O.R. killed; 5 O.R. wounded; 1 O.R. wounded at duty.	
			2 O.R. admitted hospital (sick)	WD1
	25/12/17		Holiday yesterday. Enemy fired huts at CHRDOEN CAMP (B.18 a 9.7) injuring 1	
			Accommodation in CHIDAE TRENCH (C.9 a 8.7)	
			Casualties: 1 O.R. (Lutner Copl 1/7 Bn Argyll) wounded	
			2 O.R. wounded hospital (sick) 3 O.R. (other ranks) attached Repton (?) wounded	WD1
			Sections 1 + 3 not attached General (? ?) 1st C.L.R. moved from CAMZ SAM (? ? ? ?)	WD1
			CHIDAE TRENCH (C.9 a 8.7)	
			1 Pioneer (attached) wounded	WD1
	26/12/17		Hicks k. yesterday	WD1
			do	
	26/12/17		For 24th Sections Succession to CHIDAE TRENCH to relieve the 1 + 3 Sections to attend to Gravel Road 7/R, 7/6th Sapping Platoons relieved 9th + 16th Platoons in MINE E	WD1
			TRENCH	
			Work - WATER HOUSES. Recovering tin and covering rifle huts ; building down concertinas wire in front of	WD1

Nº 51154 FIELD COMPANY, R.E.

WAR DIARY
INTELLIGENCE SUMMARY
(Erase heading not required.)

Army Form C. 2118.

Instructions regarding War Diaries and Intelligence Summaries are contained in F.S. Regs., Part II. and the Staff Manual respectively. Title pages will be prepared in manuscript.

Place	Date	Hour	Summary of Events and Information	Remarks and references to Appendices
Map S. 28 (BELGIUM)	26/12/17 (cont^d)		LANGEMARCK road to "A" track; improving rifle pits and excavating for shelters at SENEGAL FARM; extending rifle pits at TAUBE FARM; repairs to duckboard track in neighbourhood of CONDÉ FARM; thickening & extending wire in front of MAIN LINE, TAUBE, SENEGAL FARMS; supervision of Infantry carrying parties R.E. materials ENGLE Switch — SENEGAL FARM; wiring in front of Long Point forward Line.	
			U.24.c.5.9. U.17.d.1.3	
			Casualties — 2 O.R. (Sappers) admitted hospital (sick)	5.14.K.
	27/12/17		Works — laying in front of Corps line improvement of rifle pits at SENEGAL FARM, TAUBE FARM & HORSE HOUSES. Supervision of Infantry carrying parties as yesterday; wiring in front of COMPROMIS FARM-STRING HOUSE M.G.; extending & thickening Wire at TAUBE FARM; Repairing MILLER'S HOUSE MEBUS (V.13.a.3.6). 1 Section employed on work in Camp.	
			5 L.D. Horses and 1 Mule evacuated, sick to Divisional Mobile Veterinary Section (by strength)	5.14.K.
	28/12/17		Works — Wiring in front of Corps Line & COMPROMIS FARM — STRING HOUSES, improvement of Infantry cover, further drainage of MILLER'S HOUSE MEBUS and improvement of rifle pits at SENEGAL FARM all as yesterday. Work on Long Points at U.17.d.1.3 & U.24.c.2.9; reinforcing duckboard tracks (A.S.R. 1 (appendices)) improvement of rifle pits at COMPROMIS FARM. (U.12.b.1.3.); thickening & strengthening buried cable near Long SWITCH FARM — WATER HOUSES, improving stables & accommodation at Long Horse Lane (B.30.a.9.3).	K.14.L

WAR DIARY
INTELLIGENCE SUMMARY.
(Erase heading not required.)

Army Form C. 2118.

Instructions regarding War Diaries and Intelligence Summaries are contained in F.S. Regs., Part II. and the Staff Manual respectively. Title pages will be prepared in manuscript.

511th FIELD COMPANY, R.E.

No..........
Date..........

Place	Date	Hour	Summary of Events and Information	Remarks and references to Appendices
Map 28 BELGIUM	28/10/17		Reinforcement sub received from R.E. Base Depot.	1544
	29/10/17		Working party of 2 Corpls & 20 O.R. working on "Pill Box" at CORDRUCHE FARM. Improvement to dug outs & Camp.	
			Section drainage of MINERS HOUSE TRACKS. Improvement to 3 Coy Horse Lines & maintenance of mill.	
			Company all in yesterday. Working in front of CORBROCIS FARM, CORDRUGE HOUSE (NH & C.L.O.) cleaning out	
			Pill Box at SONNERM FARM; clearing out and draining works before at TWIGE FARM; strengthening	
			decauville wire in front of TWIGE FARM; laying & maintaining light railway siding at South Siding in	
			BANGALORE.	W.T.K.
			O.C. reported to Bureau at R.E. School of Instruction, BLENDECQUES (near ST.OMER).	
	30/10/17		Work - strengthening of cam horse lines (B.30.a.9.3) and maintenance of duckboard tracks as yesterday.	
			Preparing accommodation at CANDLE TRENCH (C.4..-. #7). Spraying stand-by in horsetrance framework	
			from BARD CAUSEWAY to HAYMARKET DUMP. As much possible to shelter & rest in huts near by.	
			Return of O.C.E. 173rd Brigade.	R.T.K.
	31/10/17		No. 4 Section relieved from CANDLE TRENCH to CANAL BANK (C.13 c 3 6).	
			No. 2 section relieved from CANDLE TRENCH to CANAL BANK + 2/Lts & 2/Lts Sapping Platoons to Hull's Shelter on	
			relief by Nos 1 & 3 sections and 2/5 & 2/6 Sapping Platoons	
			Work - Maintenance of duckboard tracks as yesterday. Strengthening wire in front of TWIGE FM	W.T.K.

/ Army Form C. 2118.

WAR DIARY
INTELLIGENCE SUMMARY.
(Erase heading not required.)

Place	Date	Hour	Summary of Events and Information	Remarks and references to Appendices
Map 28 BELGIUM.	31/9/17		Raining to all Masses at TAUBE FARM; digging rifle pits and excavating for and erecting small elephant shelters. SENEGAL FARM; shaving shelters at MILLARS HOUSE; erecting shelters & rifle pits COMPROMIS FARM; wiring COMPROMIS FARM–COURAGE HOUSE; improvement of Nearby carrying parties; thickening wire in front of hop-peline. One station employed in Cent 3 with the	

511 2nd Coy
Vol 13

511th (LONDON) Field Co R.E.

WAR - DIARY

1st - 31st January 1918.

9

WAR DIARY / INTELLIGENCE SUMMARY

Army Form C. 2118.

Place	Date	Hour	Summary of Events and Information	Remarks and references to Appendices
Map 28. N.W.	1/1/18		Works:- TAUBE FARM - Erecting wire and cleaning out MEBUS; SENEGAL FARM - Erecting trench shelters and small English shelters; digging rifle pits; MILLER'S HOUSE MEBUS - Drainage; COMPROMIS FARM - Erecting shelters in rifle pits; wiring in front of farm; STRING HOUSES - Repairing damaged wire and erection of new wire. CORPS LINE - Setting out new wire; digging and revetting localities. Supervision of Infantry burying parties; MURAT CAMP (B.30.a.9.3.) - erecting NISSEN hut. 1 O.R. arrived as reinforcement from R.E. Base Depot.	WTK
	2/1/18		Works:- Work on TAUBE FARM - STRING HOUSES LINE and on CORPS LINE as yesterday. MURAT CAMP - erecting curling walls to shelters. Maintenance of "A", "B" and LANGEMARCK Duckboard Tracks.	WTK
	3/1/18		All work as yesterday.	WTK
	4/1/18		No.2 Section & 275th Sapping Platoon relieved No.1 Section and 275th Sapping Platoon at CANDLE TRENCH (C.9.a.4.) Works:- Work on TAUBE FARM - STRING HOUSES LINE as yesterday, with addition of flanking bays to WATER HOUSES & COMPROMIS FARM. Other work as yesterday. 2 O.R. attached to Hq/rs 58th Divn. for duty and rations.	WTK
	5/1/18		No.4 Section & 2/10th Sapping Platoon relieved No.3 Section and 2/6th Sapping Platoon at CANDLE TRENCH. Warning Order with reference to Rams of Regt. received from C.R.E. 58th Division. Works:- Work on TAUBE FARM - STRING HOUSES LINE as yesterday, with addition of flanking bays to STRING HOUSES. Corps Line Wiring. Erecting corrugated iron cover to tanks at Divisional Baths near ESSEX FARM (C.25.a.6.7.)	WTK

Army Form C. 2118.

WAR DIARY
INTELLIGENCE SUMMARY
(Erase heading not required.)

Instructions regarding War Diaries and Intelligence Summaries are contained in F. S. Regs., Part II. and the Staff Manual respectively. Title pages will be prepared in manuscript.

Place	Date	Hour	Summary of Events and Information	Remarks and references to Appendices
Map 28 N.W.	5/1/18 (cont.)		WORKS (cont'd) - MURAT CAMP - Building splinter-proof wall round stable.	WD.1
	6/1/18		1 Rider and 2 L.D. Horses evacuated to Mobile Veterinary Section (off strength).	
			Works :- V.13.c.5.8. - revetting 3 rifle pits. Work on TAUBE FARM - SPRING HOUSES LINE. Divisional Baths and MURAT CAMP as yesterday. Supervision of Infantry Carrying Parties.	WD.1
	7/1/18		Nos. 2 & 4 Sections returned from CANDLE TRENCH to CANAL BANK. 174th Infantry Brigade sapping Platoons returned to respective Battalions.	
			Officer of 203 Field Coy. R.E. attended with reference to handing over of work.	
			2. BR. returned to Unit from attachment to Divisional Headquarters.	
			Works :- Maintenance of "A", "B" and LANGEMARCK Buckboard tracks; strengthening and thickening work in front of Corps Line (Rest Sector). Work on Divisional Baths completed.	WD.1
	8/1/18		Notification received in Divisional Routine Orders of award of Military Cross to O.C. Company.	
			Lieut. F.P. HUGHES admitted to II Corps Rest Station.	
			Works and Transport Lines handed over to 203 Field Coy. R.E. Billets in CANAL BANK handed over to 503 Field Coy. R.E. Company moved from Billets at CANAL BANK and BRIELEN to BRIGADE TRAIN CAMP.	
Map. 27.			(L.27.A.6.2. Map 27). Captain LACE remained to conduct Officers of 203 Field Coy. R.E. round works.	WD.1

Army Form C. 2118.

WAR DIARY
INTELLIGENCE SUMMARY
(Erase heading not required.)

Instructions regarding War Diaries and Intelligence Summaries are contained in F. S. Regs., Part II. and the Staff Manual respectively. Title pages will be prepared in manuscript.

Place	Date	Hour	Summary of Events and Information	Remarks and references to Appendices
Prop. 27.	9/1/19.		Improvement of Camp accommodation, including bunking of Nissen huts. Captain LACE rejoined Unit.	W.H.L.
	10/1/18		Lieut. DAVIDSON rejoined Unit from on leave to U.K. Lieut. HUGHES returned from II Corps Rest Station. Inspection of rifles, box respirators & P.H. Helmets. Improvement of Camp accommodation.	W.H.L.
	11/1/18		Lieut. HUGHES proceeded on leave to U.K. Squad and Coy. Drill. Special instruction for N.C.O's class. Improvement of Camp accommodation	W.H.L.
	12/1/18		As yesterday. 2. O.R. admitted hospital.	W.H.L.
	13/1/18		Church Parade. 3. O.R. admitted hospital. 6. O.R. attached for duty and rations to 2/4th Battn. R.F. Regt. for work on Gasboard at D.30.a.O.1.	W.S.H.
	14/1/18		Squad & Company & Rifle Drill; Special instruction for N.C.Os. Route March. 1. O.R. transferred to Transportation Troops Base Depôt.	W.H.L.
	15/1/18		No 1 Section - Repairing & improving bayonet-fighting Course at F.27.a.3.5. No 2 & 4 Sections - Training in pontoon and trestle bridging. No 3 Section - Improving Camp accommodation; lecture on pontoon bridging. Warning Order received from C.R.E. 58th Division for move to New Area.	W.H.L.

WAR DIARY / INTELLIGENCE SUMMARY

Army Form C. 2118.

Place	Date	Hour	Summary of Events and Information	Remarks and references to Appendices
Had. 27.	15/4/18		Lieut. AVIS and party proceeded to CAESTRE and received 8 L.D. horses as remounts, also 5 L.D. horses for WESSEX Field Coy. R.E. to be retained and held by 511 Field Co. pending collection.	ASH L
	16/4/18		Advance Party, under Lieut. CANNING, proceeded to VILLERS BRETTONNEUX to take over billets in new area.	
			No. 1 Section - Work on bayonet-fighting course as yesterday.	
			No. 2nd Section - Training in Trestle and Pontoon Bridging and in wiring.	
			No. 4 Section - Repairs to Hutting, after storm of previous night.	
			1 O.R. admitted to Hospital (Sick). 3 O.R. discharged Hospital. 1 O.R. evacuated to C.C.S. (off strength). 1 O.R. attached to C.E. Fourth Army for duty returns.	ASH L
	17/4/18		No. 1 Section - Work on bayonet-fighting course as yesterday. Remainder of Coy.- tactical training in pontooning, knots & lashings, and setting out trenches. Company Saluted.	
			Part of Coy. animals dipped.	ASH L
	18/4/18		Remainder of Coy. animals dipped.	
			6 O.R. returned from attachment to 2/11th Battalion Ch. Regt. after work on new ground.	
			No. 1 Section - Work on bayonet-fighting course as yesterday. Nos. 2 & 3 Sections - loading of Coy. Transport.	
			No. 4 Section - Lecture and instruction in wiring.	
			2 L.D. horses handed over to 503 Field Co. R.E. & 3 L.D. horses handed to 504 Field Co.	ASH L

WAR DIARY / INTELLIGENCE SUMMARY.

Army Form C. 2118.

(Erase heading not required.)

Instructions regarding War Diaries and Intelligence Summaries are contained in F. S. Regs., Part II. and the Staff Manual respectively. Title pages will be prepared in manuscript.

Place	Date	Hour	Summary of Events and Information	Remarks and references to Appendices
Map 27. R.a.b AMIENS.	19/4/18		Company march from PROVEN Area entrained at PROVEN and detrained at VILLERS BRETONNEUX	A.J.H.Q
	20/4/18		Company arrived at VILLERS BRETONNEUX and proceeded by march route to CASTEL.	1.H.Q
	21/4/18		O.C. rejoined Unit after lectures at R.E. School of Instruction BLENDECQUES.	
			1. O.R. evacuated to B.C.L. (off strength).	13.H.Q
			Inspection of Rifles, box respirators and P.H. Helmets. Digging latrines and improving billets.	
	22/4/18		Squad company, extended order and rifle drill. Washing vehicles and preparing targets for rifle range. Special class of instruction for N.C.Os.	
			Instructions received from G. Ra 58th Division for O.C. to assume duties as Acting C.R.E. during absence of Field Companies to ERCHEU Area.	13.H.Q
	23/4/18		O.C. attended Headquarters 58th Division, CORBIE, in connection with move to new area.	
			Advance Party proceeded to ROSIÈRES.	21.H.Q
	24/4/18		Squad, company and rifle drill. Target practice at improvised range.	
			Company moved by march route to ROSIÈRES. Advance party proceeded from ROSIÈRES to ROYE.	1.H.Q
			8. O.R. attached to 174th Brigade for instructional purpose.	
	25/4/18		Company moved by march route from ROSIÈRES to ROYE.	
			Lieut. AVIS proceeded on leave to U.K. 1. O.R. returned from R.E. Base Depot.	M.H.Q

WAR DIARY

INTELLIGENCE SUMMARY.
(Erase heading not required.)

Army Form C. 2118.

Place	Date	Hour	Summary of Events and Information	Remarks and references to Appendices
Nr AMIENS	26/1/18		Lieut. LYON attached to C.R.E. 53rd Division for duty as Acting Adjutant.	
			Advance Party proceeded to FRENICHES to arrange with 21st Infantry Brigade for billets for Company at GOLANCOURT.	
			Company moved by march route from ROYE to GOLANCOURT.	A.M.1
Nr ST QUENTIN	27/1/18		Company moved by march route, with 21st Infantry Brigade, from GOLANCOURT to GRANDRU.	
	28/1/18		O.C. reported to Commandant du Génie at ROUEZ to reconnoitre work in line.	
			Advance party proceeded to ROUEZ to take over billets at ROUEZ and LIEZ.	A.M.1
			Company rested.	
			2. O.R. arrived from R.E. Base Depôt as reinforcements.	
	29/1/18		Company moved by march route from GRANDRU to ROUEZ.	
			Sections 3 and 4 proceeded from ROUEZ to LIEZ.	A.M.1
Nr Mat 66C SW 30/1/18 Edition 2.A.	30/1/18		O.C. reconnoitred forward area and work in line.	
			Section No1 and No2. Work at ROUEZ FARM. Clearing and disinfecting Horse Standings and making and erecting latrines.	
			Section No3. Digging Trenches on Third Switch line at N.15.c.1.6 to N.17.c.4.7 (NIGHT).	
			Section No4. Cleaning and improving billets and making and erecting latrines.	R.H.2

Army Form C. 2118.

WAR DIARY
INTELLIGENCE SUMMARY
(Erase heading not required.)

Place	Date	Hour	Summary of Events and Information	Remarks and references to Appendices
Map Sht 45W. Sheet 2A.	31/1/18		Sections No1 and No3. Carried on with work as yesterday.	
			Section No3. Digging trenches on third sketch line (N17d.4.7. to N17a.6.2.)(NIGHT).	
			Section No4. Working Dug Outs at FORT VENDEUIL and in second sketch line at N17c.10.45	N.A.H.
			Instructions received to move H.Q and Section No1. on 12/2/18 from ROUEZ to LIEZ.	

A6945 Wt. W14422/M1160 350,000 12/16 D. D. & L. Forms/C./2118/14

S/11 Field C° R.E.
Volume B

WAR DIARY
or
INTELLIGENCE SUMMARY
(Erase heading not required.)

Army Form C. 2118.

Place	Date	Hour	Summary of Events and Information	Remarks and references to Appendices
Map Sheet 66 d S.W. New 2A	1/2/18		Headquarters and N°1 Section moved from Rouez to Liez.	
			1. O.R. arrived as reinforcement from R.E. Base Depôt.	
			Works :- N°1 Section :- Improving accommodation at Liez, N.31.d.8.2.	
			N°2 Section :- Lowering grenade shelters at Divisional Grenade Store, S.22.a.9.9.; dismantling horse standings and making & erecting latrines at Rouez Farm and Rouez, S.27.a.1.0.	
			N°3 Section :- Digging trenches in 3rd Switch Line, N.17.a.8.2. to N.17.c.2.7.; preparing line of wire N.18.a.7.6 to N.18.a.6.7.	
			N°4 Section :- Construction of two dugouts at Fort Vendeuil. N.18.c.2.5.	MHR
	2/2/18		N°1 Section :- Wiring 3rd Switch Line at N.17.a.	
			N°3 Section :- Work on trenches in 3rd Switch Line as yesterday; N°s 2 & 4 Sections :- works as yesterday.	MHR
	3/2/18		N°s 1, 2 & 3 Sections :- Work as yesterday. N°4 Section :- Construction of 2 dugouts at Fort Vendeuil; construction of dugout for Artillery at N.16.d.8.3.; repairing screens on side of Liez - Fort Vendeuil Road.	MHR
	4/2/18		N°1 Section :- Draining and excavating N°2 Post in front of Switch Line. N°2 Section :- Work as yesterday; also improving R.A. hut, Rouez. N°3 Section :- Digging trenches on 3rd Switch Line N.16.b.7.2. & N.16.b.1.3.; erecting wire entanglements on 3rd Switch Line, N.17.d.8.7. to N.17.a.5.8. N°4 Section :- Work as yesterday.	MHR
	5/2/18		Lieut. Davidson met C.E. III Corps with reference to taking charge of work in Battle Zone on 175th Brigade Sector.	

WAR DIARY
INTELLIGENCE SUMMARY
(Erase heading not required.)

Army Form C. 2118.

Place	Date	Hour	Summary of Events and Information	Remarks and references to Appendices
Map Sheet 66° S.W. Edition 2D	5/2/18		No 1 Section :- Accounting for drawing and wiring Posts VENDEUIL; No 2 Section :- Taking down Adrian Huts at S.27.a.9.3 and preparing site for re-erection at S.27.a.0.1.; No 3 Section :- Digging trenches on 3rd Zurich Line N.16.4.1.3.6 N.16.d.0.4.; erecting wire entanglements N.17.d.5.8 & N.17.d.3.7. No 4 Section :- Work as yesterday.	WAR
	6/2/18		2 Remounts (Riders) received. No 1 Section :- Work as yesterday. No 2 Section :- Re-erection of Adrian Hut at S.27.a.0.1.; making notice boards and improvement of R.A. & Divisional Billets. No 3 Section :- Making hurdles at R.E. Dump, LIEZ. No 4 Section :- Continuing of 2 dugouts at FORT VENDEUIL & of deep dugout for Artillery continued as yesterday; sinking shaft for deep dugout N.16.d.5.9. O.C. visited Boehn Line with No. 1 Section and Lieut. DAVIDSON.	WAR
	7/2/18		Lieut. CANNING nominated to take charge of Demolition of Bridges in Corps Area; O.C. Lieut. CANNING inspected bridges for which Company is responsible. No 1 Section :- Accounting trauerse and fire trench and revetting latter at No 1 Post (1st Line VENDEUIL Switch). No 3 Section :- Completing & improving wire entanglements on 3rd Zurich Line. No 2 & 4th Sections - Work as yesterday.	WAR
	8/2/18		1 O.R. proceeded on Course at Fifth Army Infantry School; 2 O.R. returned to Coy. from attachment to 174th Infantry Brigade. No 1 Section :- Improving No. 2 Post and improving wire in front of No 3 Post (1st Line VENDEUIL Switch); No 3 Section - Work on wire entanglements as yesterday; digging trench on 3rd Zurich Line; setting out Posts in Battle Zone. No 2 & 4th Sections - Work as yesterday.	WAR

Army Form C. 2118.

WAR DIARY
INTELLIGENCE SUMMARY
(Erase heading not required.)

Place	Date	Hour	Summary of Events and Information	Remarks and references to Appendices
Map Sheet 66cSW Edition 2.	9/2/18		6. OR. returned to Coy. from attachment to 175th Infantry Brigade.	
			No.1 Section:- 1st Line VENDEUIL Switch:- Drawing and improving No.2 Post; excavating for fire bay No.2 Post; No.2 Section:- Work as yesterday; also construction of Boat. No.3 Section:- Erecting wire entanglements, 3rd Switch line; setting out posts in Battle Zone. No.4 Section:- Work as yesterday; also repairs to LIEZ-FORT VENDEUIL Road.	MHR
	10/2/18.		G.O.C. 58th Division, G.O.C. 175th Brigade, G.S.O.1 and S.O.R.E. visited Battle Zone with O.C. and issued instructions as to position of Section Posts in Battle Zone.	
			No.1 Section:- Excavating traverse at end of No.2 Post, other work as yesterday. No.2 Section:- work on erection of Adrian Hut as yesterday; also making and painting notice-boards; No.3 Section:- Work as yesterday; also digging trenches in 3rd Switch Line. No.4 Section:- Work as yesterday; also making puddles at R.E. Dump, LIEZ.	
			A.S.C. personnel attached and train wagon returned to A.S.C. Coy.	
			Lieut. AUER rejoined Unit from leave to U.K.	
			2/Lieut. ANDERSON and 2/Lieut. CONSTABLE promoted to rank of Corporal, each with effect from 1/2/18	MHR
	11/2/18		Captain LACE proceeded on leave to U.K. 1 N.C.O. & 4 Sappers attached for duty and rations to 2/10th Battalion.	
			C.E. Regiment; 1. OR. rejoined Unit from No.12 Stationary Hospital.	
			No.1 Section:- Work continued on No. 1 & 2. Posts; also excavating for fire-trays & traverse, 1st Line VENDEUIL Switch.	
			No.2 Section:- Work on erection of Adrian Hut as yesterday. No.3 Section:- Setting out posts in Battle Zone;	MHR

WAR DIARY / INTELLIGENCE SUMMARY

Army Form C. 2118.

Place	Date	Hour	Summary of Events and Information	Remarks and references to Appendices
Map Sheet 66 S.W. Edition 2.d	11/2/18 (2pm)		No Section (Cav): Levelling parapet and stripping sam, also erecting wire entanglements 3rd Switch Line.	
			No. 4 Section: Work as yesterday.	MAP
	12/2/18		Lieut AVIS attached to 503 Field Co R.E. 1 O.R. evacuated to No. 40 C.C.S. (off strength)	
			No. 1 Section: Drainage and improvement of No. 1 & 2 Pets. 1st Line VENDEUIL switch. No. 2 Section: Erection of Addison Hut continued: also erection of small hut, trestle and stores; No. 3 Section: Work on 3rd Switch Line & wiring as yesterday; repairing camouflage fence along road. No. 4 Section: Repair of LIEZ - FORT - de VENDEUIL Road, drainage and improvement of deep dugout at FORT VENDEUIL; improving same in front of 3rd Switch Line.	MAP
			Instructions received to work on Battle Zone and VENDEUIL switch line to be handed over to 92nd Field Coy. R.E.	
	13/2/18		No. 2 Section: Erection of huts as yesterday; erection of splinter-proof wall at Div! Headquarters. No. 3 Section:- softening work in Battle Zone to choro of 92nd Field Coy. R.E. & officers of 55th Infantry Brigade; taking platoon points on ground and digging trenches in battle zone. No. 4 Section: Repair of road as yesterday; preparing bridge in Brigade area over St QUENTIN CANAL for demolition.	MAP
	14/2/18		1 O.R. attached to 58th Division "Q" for duty. 1 O.R. proceeded on leave at Fifth Army Sanitary School. No. 1 Section:- Reconstruction of ferry at Broken Bridge at O.30.a.6.1; No. 3 Section:- Setting out platoon points and communication trenches in Battle Zone. Nos. 2 & 4 Sections:- Work as yesterday.	MAP
			Instructions received for move of Coy. on 15th instant from LIEZ to MENNESSIS.	

Army Form C. 2118.

WAR DIARY
or
INTELLIGENCE SUMMARY.
(Erase heading not required.)

Instructions regarding War Diaries and Intelligence Summaries are contained in F. S. Regs., Part II, and the Staff Manual respectively. Title pages will be prepared in manuscript.

Place	Date	Hour	Summary of Events and Information	Remarks and references to Appendices
Map Sheet 66 e S.W Position 2 A.	15/2/18		Headquarters and sections 1, 3 and 4 moved to MENNESSIS (M.36.d.7.9).	
			1. O.R. evacuated to Casualty Clearing Station (off strength).	
			No. 2 Section:- Work as yesterday; also clearing dug-out in wood at S.27.c.5.9. No. 3 Section & part No.1 Section - Setting out and supervising work in Battle Zone; work in Battle Zone finally handed over to 92nd Field Company R.E.	
			No. 4 & Lieut. No.1 Section:- Preparation for demolition of bridges over St. Quentin Canal, repairs to LIEZ - FORT VENDEUIL Road.	M.R.
	16/2/18	1.55pm	Rehearsal carried out of demolition of Bridges.	
			No.1 Section :- Improving shelters and accommodation at VENDEUIL; erecting billet accommodation at MENNESSIS VILLAGE (M.36.A. & a); No. 2 Section :- Work as yesterday. No.3 Section - Work as No.1 Section above. No. 4 Section - Work as yesterday.	
			2. O.R. attached to Headquarters 58th Divisional Engineers for duty.	M.R.
			O.C. & Lieut. HUGHES started work in Zone.	
	17/2/18		1. O.R. rejoined unit from Fifth Army Sanitary School. 3. O.R. joined Unit as reinforcements from R.E. Base Depot.	
			No.1 Section & parts of Nos. 3 & 4 Sections - Improving shelters and revetting trenches right of Brigade Sector; erecting and improving billet accommodation at MENNESSIS. No. 2 Section - Work as yesterday. No. 3 Section :- Repairing road between REMIGNY - VENDEUIL Road. No.4 Section - Road repairs as yesterday; constructing deep dug-out at FORT VENDEUIL	M.R.
	18/2/18		Second rehearsal of demolition of Bridges. Lieut. HUGHES & 15. O.R. of No.1 Section to forward billets at QUARRY.	
			No.1 Section :- Making 2 passes over OISE River opposite QUARRY. No. 2 & 4 Sections - Work as yesterday.	

WAR DIARY
INTELLIGENCE SUMMARY

(Erase heading not required.)

Army Form C. 2118.

Place	Date	Hour	Summary of Events and Information	Remarks and references to Appendices
Map Sheet 66^c. S.W. Position 2A.	18/3/18	(Con-id)	No 3 Section :- Erection of shelters and accommodation at 175th Brigade Transport Lines, L.1152; improving shelters and accommodation at VENDEUIL; preparing material for gallery at FORT VENDEUIL.	
	19/3/18		No. 3 Section proceeded to billets + for work at ROUEZ, and No. 2 Section to MENNESSIS.	WAR
			O.C. met C.R.E. 58th Division at MENNESSIS.	
			No 1 Section :- Work as yesterday, also improvement of billets at MENNESSIS. No. 3 Section :- Erection of splinter-proof walling at Rouez billets; erecting hut for signals. No 2 Section :- Work as yesterday; also improvement of shelters and accommodation and revetting trenches at VENDEUIL.	MHP
	20/3/18		O.C., Lieut. CANNING and 175th Brigade M.G. Officer reconnoitred for site for M.G. emplacements in front of VENDEUIL FORT.	
			No. 1 Section - Completion of ferries over Oise River; improving shelters at right of Brigade Sector; protecting dugouts at VENDEUIL FORT and VILLAGE against gas. No. 2 Section - Repairing rile for Pioneer Camp at Bois du MOULINET (T.8.b.8.9); improving accommodation at MENNESSIS; erecting huts at Battalion Headquarters, BOIS-DE-VIEVILLE (N.25.b.5.5.); improving accommodation at MENNESSIS. No. 3 Section - Work as yesterday; also excavating for O.P. for Signals. No^o 4 Section - Work as yesterday.	
	21/3/18		O.C. with C.O. 2/12th Battalion, reconnoitred for Battle Headquarters for Left Battalion 175th Brigade in locality of N.26.a.2.8.	
			No 1 Section - Preparing material for footbridge over Oise River at QUARRY; protection of dugouts against gas as yesterday; improving billet accommodation at MENNESSIS.	

Army Form C. 2118.

WAR DIARY
INTELLIGENCE SUMMARY

(Erase heading not required.)

Instructions regarding War Diaries and Intelligence Summaries are contained in F. S. Regs., Part II. and the Staff Manual respectively. Title pages will be prepared in manuscript.

Place	Date	Hour	Summary of Events and Information	Remarks and references to Appendices
Map Sheet 66c.S.W. Position 2.A	21/2/18	(contd)	No 2 Section:- Work on General Camp and erection of huts as yesterday; also improving shelters on Right of Brigade Sector. No 3 Section:- Improving billets, excavation for Brigade O.P. work on Signals dugout and splinter-proof walling as yesterday. No 4 Section:- Repairs to road as yesterday; Construction of deep dugout at Fort VENDEUIL.	Nil
	22/2/18		O.C. went round works with C.R.E. and reconnoitred for sites for M.G. emplacements in front of VENDEUIL. L.C.R. detached to Headquarters 58th Divl. Engineers for duty. 1/c O.R. returned hoof. for attachment to 2/4th Batt. C.L. Regt. No 1 Section:- Work as yesterday; also supervision of excavation for R.A.M.C. Collecting Post at Railway Cutting. MENNESSIS; No 2 Section:- Work on General Camp and erection of huts as yesterday; cutting and revetting steps at 175th Brigade Headquarters, improving billets at Mennessis; No 3 & 4 Sections:- Work as yesterday.	Nil
	23/2/18		O.C. visited C.R.E. at ROUEZ. Instructions received to hand over work in progress to 92nd Field Coy. R.E. and for move of Company to PIERREMANDE, two lorries to proceed to billets at CARRIERES-BERNAGOUSSE. No 1 Section:- Work on preparation of footbridges as yesterday; excavation for R.A.M.C. Collecting Post; improving accommodation at MENNESSIS. No 2 Section:- Work as yesterday. at FORT VEZ. No 3 & 4 Sections:- Work as yesterday.	"Nil"
	24/2/18		Work handed over to 92nd Field Co. R.E.; OC 511 Field Co. went round works with OC 92 Field Coy. R.E.	Nil

WAR DIARY or INTELLIGENCE SUMMARY

Army Form C. 2118.

Place	Date	Hour	Summary of Events and Information	Remarks and references to Appendices
Map Sheet 66.S.W. Gillham 2.A.	24/9/18		Lieuts. HARVEY and HUGHES with 8. O.R. proceeded as Advance Party to Rear Area.	
			Inspection by D.D.M.S. 58th Division of 3. O.R. for medical reclassification. 1. O.R. returned to Unit from attachment	
			to Headquarters, 58th Divisional Engineers.	
			No 1 Section – Repairing up bridge for OISE River; No 3 Section – Works as yesterday; No 4 Section – Apportioning	
			materials and fixing demolition charges at Bridges.	MHR
Map 70 D.N.W.	25/9/18		O.C. proceeded to Headquarters 58th Divisional Engineers to take over duties of C.R.E.	
			Work and Billets handed over to 92nd Field Coy. R.E.	
			Company march from CAMP to PIERREMANDE (G.28.d.2.8.) Advance Party of No 2 Section to CARRIERES BERNAGOUSSE.	
			2 O.R. attached to Headquarters 58th Divisional Engineers	MHR
			No 2 Section proceeded to billets and work at CARRIERES BERNAGOUSSE.	
	26/9/18		Lieut. CANNING went ahead with O.C. 504 Field Coy R.E. in connection with taking over C.R.E. and Adjutants	
			duties from Headquarters, PIERREMANDE.	
			1. O.R. attached 58th Divisional Engineers Headquarters for duty and rations.	
			No 1 Section – Conducting parties into Battle Zone; No 2 Section – Working at CARRIERES BERNAGOUSSE;	
			No 3 Section – Taking up work in Battle Zone; No 4 Section – Work on R.E. Dump and on billets in	
			PIERREMANDE.	MHR

WAR DIARY
INTELLIGENCE SUMMARY.
(Erase heading not required.)

Army Form C. 2118.

Instructions regarding War Diaries and Intelligence Summaries are contained in F. S. Regs., Part II. and the Staff Manual respectively. Title pages will be prepared in manuscript.

Place	Date	Hour	Summary of Events and Information	Remarks and references to Appendices
Hupstrict 70.D.N.W.	27/9/18	—	3 O.R. returned to R.E. Base Depot for medical reclassification. 1. O.R. rejoined Unit from attachment to H.Q. 58 Divl Engineers.	
			1. O.R. admitted to No 146 F.A. on 25/9/18 (off strength)	
			Cont: Carrying inspected works in line.	
			No 1 Section: Clearing ground for wiring ROND D'ORLEANS; thinning out line of fire, H.27.a.+b; work on Heathrooke and wire entanglements. No 2 Section: Repairing chevaux de frise trenches; reconnoitring for wiring and resiting hurricade (Hill 70, H.22.b.1.8.) No 3 Section: hand digging & barricading sap trench (Hill 29, H.22.d.5.5.); preparing position for trench mortar (Hill 70, H.22.d.5.5.); trenching at BERNABOUSSE QUARRIES. No 4 Section: Protection shelters and dug-out against gas.—Right Battalion area: Construction of bathing place & wash house at PIERREMANDÉ.	N.R.
			6. O.R. attached Headquarters 58th Divisional Engineers for duty and rations.	
			No 1 Section: Construction of fire-works training in Battle zone. No 3 Section: Work as yesterday. No 4 Section:—	
28/9/18			Work as yesterday; also preparing and erecting 18-pounder gun-platforms. No 2 Section: work cancelled	
		2.50pm	Instructions received from H.R.E. to withdraw all men from works and for him to stand by at hrs headqrs ready to move at 15 minutes notice. No 2 Section and vehicles recalled to PIERREMANDÉ, and all transport loaded ready for move	N.R.

W. McCaimy Lieut Rt (T.)
for Major R.E. (T.)
Comndg 511 Field Coy. R.E.

Army Form C. 2118.

WAR DIARY
INTELLIGENCE SUMMARY
(Erase heading not required.)

Volume 14

Instructions regarding War Diaries and Intelligence Summaries are contained in F. S. Regs., Part II. and the Staff Manual respectively. Title pages will be prepared in manuscript.

511TH FIELD COMPANY

Place	Date	Hour	Summary of Events and Information	Remarks and references to Appendices
Map. 70 D.N.W. 1/20,000	1/3/18	—	Instructions of 28/2/17 to "take precautionary action" withdrawn, and orders received from C.R.E. to "resume normal conditions". No. 2 Section returned to billets at CARRIÈRES BERNAGOUSSE.	W.T.Kaw
		6.5 p.m.	Instructions received to "Man Battle Positions"; operation completed by 7.45 p.m.; normal resumed at 9.10 p.m. Works:- No. 1 Section:- Excavating to battle side of fire trenches & revetting, H.27.b.1.8. to H.27.b.2.8.; construction of breastworks, H.21.a.4. & Rond-de-l'Ennois; getting out and commencing wiring Rond d'Orleans. No. 2 Section:- Digging fire trench & wiring to right, Hill 89, H.22.d.5.5; digging communication trench to road, wiring in front of Strong Point; construction of barricade in Railway Cutting, Hill 98, H.22.b.1.8. No. 3 Section: Loading R.E. Headquarters, and improving existing accommodation. No. 4 Section: construction of shelters & dugouts against gas. Right Battalion area.	
			PIERREMANDÉ: making 18 pdr. gun platforms at R.E. Dump. Selection of clothing store for Dark House.	W.T.Kaw
	2/3/18		Captain LNCE returned to Unit from leave and took over duties as Acting O.C. Company. Works:- No. 1 Section:- Work as yesterday; also constructing breastworks at Rond d'Orleans; No. 2 Section: Wiring Battle Zone (Hills 89 & 98); preparing frames for T.M.B. emplacement. Nos. 3, 4th Sections: Works as yesterday.	L.T.H.
	3/2/18		No. 1 Section:- Wiring & construction of breastworks as yesterday; also laying duckboards. No. 2 Section: Wiring and preparation of T.M.B. fronts as yesterday; also digging fire trench Hill 98 and extension of No. 1 wiring L.G. Posts. No. 3 rd Sections:- Works as yesterday.	W.T.K.
	4/3/18		Nos. 1 & 3 Sections: Work as yesterday. No. 2 Section: Work as yesterday; also digging fire trench in Strong Point No. 1.	W.T.K.

WAR DIARY
INTELLIGENCE SUMMARY

Army Form C. 2118.

(Erase heading not required.)

Place	Date	Hour	Summary of Events and Information	Remarks and references to Appendices
Map 70.? N.W.	4/3/18		No. 4 Section:- Work as yesterday; also making NEWTON Bed for Trench Mortar & preparing reinforcement for trenches.	WJHL
	5/3/18		Other worked in line with C.R.E.	
			No.1 Section:- Wiring, revetting and laying duckboards as yesterday. No.2 Section:- Wiring Battle Zone as yesterday; also digging deep L.G. post and excavating for and placing frame for T.M. emplacements.	
			No.3 Section:- Work as yesterday. No.4 Section:- Work on NEWTON Bed as yesterday; also alteration of Lift sideway trucks for use on Decauville track; Inspection of shelters and dugouts against gas.	WJHL
	6/3/18		Nos. 1 + 2 Sections:- Work as yesterday. Nos. 3 + 4 Sections:- Work on Newton as yesterday.	WJHL
	7/3/18		Visit of Field Marshal Commanding-in-Chief to Sector.	
			1 O.R. arrived from R.E. Base Depôt as reinforcement. Casualties:- 1 O.R. Killed; 1 O.R. Wounded (at duty).	
			Work:- No.1 Section:- Constructing breastworks and wiring as yesterday; fixing one-man shelters for ammunition in breastworks. No.2 Section:- Wiring posts in Battle Zone as yesterday; digging traverse & fire trench in No.2 Post Hut 89.	
			Nos. 3+4 Sections:- Work as yesterday; supervising erection of shelters at Battle Headquarters, and repairs to dugout for M.G. Officers at CLOS-DES-VIGNES; experimenting with loopholes.	WJHL
	8/3/18		No.1 Section:- Wiring & Construction of breastworks as yesterday; construction of new Post at H.27.b.3.3. No.2 Section:- Work on Battle Zone as yesterday; also construction of T.M.B. ammunition store. No.3 Section:- Work at CLOS-DES-VIGNES as yesterday; also erecting breastwork at H.33.b.9.9; constructing Post, and thinning out line of fire at H.27.b.	WJHL

Army Form C. 2118.

WAR DIARY
or
INTELLIGENCE SUMMARY
(Erase heading not required.)

Instructions regarding War Diaries and Intelligence Summaries are contained in F. S. Regs., Part II. and the Staff Manual respectively. Title pages will be prepared in manuscript.

(3)

Place	Date	Hour	Summary of Events and Information	Remarks and references to Appendices
Map 1/20 N.W.	8/3/18		No. 4 Section:- Work on alteration of light railway tracks and gas protection of dugouts as yesterday; also construction of Battle Headquarters for R.F.A. at Sincent.	W.H.K.
	9/3/18		1 O.R. rejoined Unit as reinforcement. Lieut. HARVEY left Unit to proceed on leave to U.K. Major ROBERSON arrived at Military Cemetery, CHAUNY, A.80.d.25.90. No.3 Section proceeded to billets at CARRIERES BERNAGOUSSE, relieving No.2 Section who returned to PIERREMANDE. No.1 Section:- Wiring, construction of trenchworks and revetting as yesterday. No.3 Section:- Work as for No.2 Section in Battle Zone yesterday. No.4 Section:- Work as yesterday.	W.H.K.
	10/3/18		Nos. 1 + 2 Sections:- Work as for No.1 Section yesterday; also excavating & revetting new Post at H.27.b.2.1; tracking Chemeaux-des-Prieur. No.3 Section:- Battle Zone - wiring & digging traverse to No.2 Post; working tunnelled entrance to ammunition store; framing T.M.B. position ammunition store. No.4 Section:- Gas protection & alteration of light railway tracks as yesterday; construction of tunnelled M.G. emplacement at H.22.c.6.44; supervising erection of shelters at Battle Headquarters & repair of M.G. dugout, GROS-DES-VIGNES.	W.H.K.
	11/3/18		Nos. 1 + 2 Sections:- Work as yesterday; also constructing new Post at H.27.b.5.5. No.3 Section:- Battle Zone - wiring and framing T.M.B. store as yesterday. No.4 Section:- Construction of tunnelled M.G. emplacement as yesterday; also gas protection; making sand cases for front posts.	W.H.K.
	12/3/18		Casualty: 1 O.R. wounded in action.	W.H.K.

Army Form C. 2118.

WAR DIARY
or
INTELLIGENCE SUMMARY

(Erase heading not required.)

Instructions regarding War Diaries and Intelligence Summaries are contained in F. S. Regs., Part II. and the Staff Manual respectively. Title pages will be prepared in manuscript.

Place	Date	Hour	Summary of Events and Information	Remarks and references to Appendices
Map 70 D N.W.	12/3/16		Works: No. 1 & 2 Section : Rond-d'Orleans - constructing breastworks and wiring; Rond-de-L'Ennois - wiring and construction of breastworks for new posts; Caillette Trench - fixing ammunition boxes, excavating for & revetting Post at H.27.a.4.4.4.; Clos-des-Vignes - revetting post and constructing breastwork. No. 3 Section: wiring on Hill 98, and fixing T.M.B. ammunition post Hill 89. No. 4 Section: As yesterday.	WTHL
	13/3/16		No. 3 Section returned from Carrières Bernagousse to Billots at Pierremande. No. 1 & 2 Section: Work as yesterday; also work on Clos-des-Vignes as for No. 4 Section yesterday. No. 3 Section: work on Hill 89.	WTHL
	14/3/16		No. 4 Section: Work on tunnelled dugout and on protection as yesterday; No.1 & 2 Sections: Work as yesterday; also Mining out in front of fire bay, Caillette Trench. No. 3 Section: Work on Hill 89 as yesterday; Battle Zone Headquarters, H.27.a.0.1.- excavating for and fixing elephant shelters; clearing and boarding entrance to chamber for H.Q. Dugout. No. 4 Section: Work as yesterday; also making Newton T.M. platforms.	WTHL
	15/3/16		1.O.R. reported sick to hospital. No 1 & 2 Sections: Work on Rond d'Orleans & Caillette Trench and breastworks at Rond-de-L'Ennois as yesterday; constructing and wiring new posts in H.14, H.20 & H.21; revetting post at H.27 & H.4.4.4.; wiring in front of post at H.21.a.3.6.; digging & protecting new posts on Hill 75. No. 3 Section: Work on Battle Zone HQ. as yesterday; excavating for R.A.P. at Right Battalion HQ. No. 4 Section: Work as yesterday.	WTHL
	16/3/16		No. 1 Section: Work on Hill 75, H.14, H.20 & H.21 continued; thinning out wood along ray, Rond d'Orleans;	WTHL

D. D. & L., London, E.C. (A785j) Wt. W80/M1672 350,000 4/17 Sch. 59a Forms/C/2118/14

WAR DIARY

INTELLIGENCE SUMMARY

Army Form C. 2118.

Place	Date	Hour	Summary of Events and Information	Remarks and references to Appendices
Map 20 P.N.W.	16/3/18		No.1 & 2 Section: (Cont.) excavating post & wiring, ROND-de-L'EPINOIS; constructing saw post at H.27.a.8.8; filling in trench in front of wire at H.21.c; excavating rock in Post at H.27.6.9.6. No.3 Section: Work as yesterday. No.4 Section: Work on tunnelled dugout & NEWTON platforms as yesterday; erection of goo blanket frame at N.3.d.3.0 work at ROND-	
	17/3/18		No.1 & 2 Sections: Hill 75 & CAVALIERE Road - Decaunting & revetting posts & sowing side of road; work at ROND-DE-L'EPINOIS & HILL H.20 and M21 as yesterday. No.3 Section: Work as yesterday. No.4 Section: Work on tunnelled dugout & NEWTON platforms continued; fixing small elephant shelter in shell hole for M.G. emplacement; getting out spider wire maps on Hill 75. 1 O.R. returned from Course at Fifth Army Infantry School. 2 O.R. joined Unit as reinforcements. Light chestnut mare No.109 missing from H.27.a.1.3.	
	18/3/18		No.1 Section: Work on ROND-DE-L'EPINOIS & H.14.c.h. as yesterday; Hill 75 - sinking Banabuts and digging & revetting C.T. and fire trench; wiring at H.25.c.9.2. and H.27.6.0.0 to H.27.6.6.0. No.3 Section: Work as yesterday. No.4 Section: Construction of tunnelled M.G. emplacement; supervising erection of spider wire; making NEWTON T.M. platforms as yesterday; excavating for and erection of shelters for Brigade Battle Headquarters.	
	19/3/18		No.1 Section & No.2 Section: Work on H.25.c.9.2; Hill 75, ROND-DE-L'EPINOIS, H.14, H.20 & H.27 as yesterday; constructing banabuts at H.20.6.6.5; cutting tracks and fixing guide wire at H.20.6. &c. No.3 Section - Work as yesterday. No.4 Section details: Work as yesterday; also provision of goo covers at FOREMBRAY.	

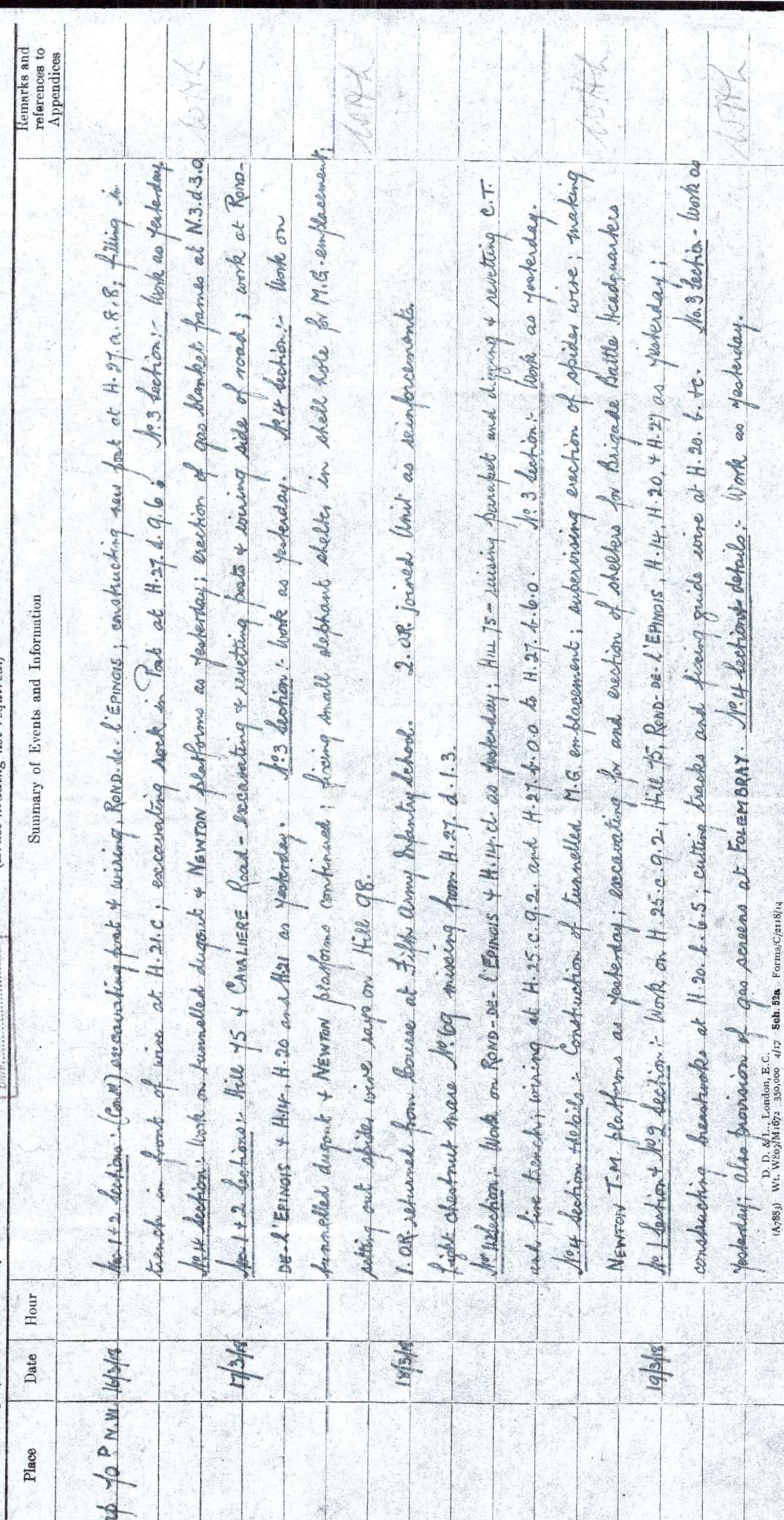

WAR DIARY or INTELLIGENCE SUMMARY

Army Form C. 2118.

(6)

Place	Date	Hour	Summary of Events and Information	Remarks and references to Appendices
Map 10.P.N.W.	20/3/18		Orders received to "Prepare for Attack". 1 O.R. evacuated to hospital.	
			Nos. 1 & 2 Sections: Laying duckboards in forts at H.u.75, clearing road for use at Rond-de-l'Epinois.	
			No.3 Section: took as yesterday. No.4 Section & Details: Work as yesterday on tunnelled M.G. emplacements, Brigade Battle Headquarters and construction of Newton Lift Sets.	15A/1
	21/3/18	6 a.m.	Orders received to "Man Battle Positions." Company standing-to.	
			No.1 Section: making register gun platforms (day). No.2 Section: Accounting for and erecting English shelters at Brigade Battle Headquarters. No.3 Section: Putting chamber frames, Newton set-beds and boxes for chamber air cylinders. No.4 Section: Preparing timber for M.G. emplacements, and opening out from gallery to permit use of M.G. at H.22.a.c.4.	15A/1 WA/1
			Nos. 1 & 3 Sections proceeded to VIRY-NOREUIL for work of digging an over-line.	
	22/3/18		Nos. 1 & 3 Sections continued work on above line as yesterday. Remainder of Coy. standing-to at PIERREMANDE, working on R.E. Dump.	
			Instructions received from C.R.E. for destruction of valuable stores at R.E. Dump in the event of evacuation of PIERREMANDE. No.4 Section returned to PIERREMANDE.	15A/1
	23/3/18		Nos. 1 & 3 Sections billeting in Railway Cutting near HILL 98.	
~~CHERISY BEAUCOURT~~				

WAR DIARY
INTELLIGENCE SUMMARY
(Erase heading not required.)

Army Form C. 2118.

Place	Date	Hour	Summary of Events and Information	Remarks and references to Appendices
Sheets 70 D.N.W & 70 E.	23/3/18		Instructions received from C.R.E. to send Officer & Sappers to Canal Bridge No.63 (L.No.a.2.5) to take over from 155 A.T. Coy. demolition stores and responsibility for destruction of Bridges 43, 44, 45, 47, 61, 63 & 64; Lieut Davidson and No.2 Section proceeded to to Bac d'ARBLINCOURT for this duty. Nos 1 & 3 Sections - Work on Green Line.	15/4/18
	24/3/18		Camp shelled by H.V. gun; transport lines removed to BAC D'ARBLINCOURT (L.23.b.9.7). No.1 Section: Construction of Strong Points on Hill 75. No.3 Section: Standing by for demolition of Bridges. No.3 & Part No.4 Sections: Improvement of defences on Green Line; remainder of No.4 Section constructing chambers for tunnelled dugout at H.22.a.6.4.	10/4/18
			No 1-4 Sections: Wiring on Green Line (day & night). No 2 Section: As yesterday. No 3 Section: Repairing 3 bridges at MAMCAMP.	10/4/18
	25/3/18		11 O.R. rejoined Unit from attachment to Headquarters 58th Divisional Engineers. Nos 2 & 3rd Sections: Working on Green Line. No.2 Section: As yesterday. No.4 Section: Construction and repair of Bridges at M.2.C.8.3.	10/4/18
	26/3/18		Casualties. 1 O.R. killed, 4 O.R. wounded at S.T. PAUL-AUX-Bois (R.16.c.3.4). Headquarters, Nos 1 & 3 Sections & Transport Lines moved to S.T. PAUL-AUX-Bois.	10/4/18
	27/3/18		62 rejoined Unit from attachment to Headquarters 58th Divisional Engineers as Acting C.R.E. 1st Section - Work on Green Line, 174th Infantry Brigade Sector, PIERREMANDE	15/4/18

WAR DIARY
or
INTELLIGENCE SUMMARY.

Army Form C. 2118.

Place	Date	Hour	Summary of Events and Information	Remarks and references to Appendices
Sheet 10 P. N.W. and 10 E.	27/9/18		No 1 Section: Work on Posts, L'Oise and Aisne Canal Line. No 3 Section: Supervising improvement and revetting of Canal Posts. No 2 Section as yesterday.	WHK
	28/9/18		Sapper KENDALL, S.G., buried at St Paul-Aux-Bois, R.B.40.1. Captain G.H. NORRIS attached to Unit. No 1 Section: Joining on brigade front Smooter's Bank of Oise & Canal. No 2 Section as yesterday. No 3 Section as yesterday. No 4 Section as yesterday.	
	29/9/18		No 1 Section: As yesterday; also preparing for demolition bridge over Canal on night of Divisional sector. Nos 2 & 4 Sections as yesterday. No 3 Section: Taking over from and continuing work of No 2 Section on preparation and patrol of Bridges for demolition.	
	30/9/18		2nd Lieut AMS rejoined Unit from attachment to 503 Field Coy. R.E. No 4 Sections: Wiring as yesterday; constructing barrel rafts; standing by and preparing for demolition Bridge at M.9.d.1.8. No 3 Section: Improving scheme for demolition of Bridges Nos 4, 4b1 - other Bridges as yesterday. No 1 Section: Work on Luce Line as yesterday; removal of R.E. stores from Dump.	
	1/10/18		No 1 Sections: Wiring as yesterday; preparation of foot bridge over Oise & Aisne Canal at M.9.a.5.2 & M.2.d.1.1 for demolition and standing by Mine and Bridge at M.9.d.1.8. No 3 Section: Work as yesterday.	

J.J. Singleton
O.C. 511 Field Coy.

58th Div.

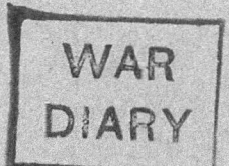

511th FIELD COMPANY, R.E.

A P R I L

1 9 1 8

WAR DIARY

INTELLIGENCE SUMMARY.

Army Form C. 2118.

Place	Date	Hour	Summary of Events and Information	Remarks and references to Appendices
Map 70 E. ST QUENTIN	1/4/18		Instructions received for move of Company from ST PAUL-AUX-BOIS to VASSENS on 2/4/18.	A.13.
	2/4/18		Preparing bridges for demolition and standing by; drainage and improvement of trenches and wiring Headquarters, Nos. 1 & 2 Sections and Transport moved by march route to VASSENS. No. 3 Section moved from Bois d'ARBLINCOURT and 4ou Section from PIERREMANDE and rejoined Company at VASSENS.	A.13. A.13.
	3/4/18		Company moved by march route from VASSENS to DOMMIERS.	A.13.
	4/4/18		Company rested during day; Transport moved at 11 p.m. Dismounted portion of Coy. at 12 midnight, proceeding to LONGPONT STATION.	A.13.
Map 62 D.	5/4/18		Company entrained at LONGPONT and proceeded to LONGUEAU Station (AMIENS). Nos. 1 & 3 Sections received at LONGUEAU for unloading of Divisional Transport. Remainder of Company marched to Camp at M.36 (near BOVES)	A.13.
	6/4/18		Nos. 1 & 3 Sections rejoined Company. Company standing by and improving billets.	A.13.
	7/4/18		Wiring, felling trees and constructing shelters and splinter-proof accommodation in Reserve Line trenches behind VILLERS BRETONNEUX	A.13.
	8/4/18		Capt. G.H. MORRIS attached to 503 Field Coy. R.E. Lieut. HASLEY & 14 O.R. rejoined Unit from leave to U.K.	A.13.
	9/4/18		Work as yesterday.	A.13.

WAR DIARY
INTELLIGENCE SUMMARY

Army Form C. 2118.

511TH FIELD COMPANY, R.E.

Place	Date	Hour	Summary of Events and Information	Remarks and references to Appendices
Map 62.D.	10/4/18		Work as yesterday.	A.9. 1.8.
	11/4/18		Work as yesterday; also making ammunition recesses and trussing wire in Support Line.	A.9. 2.
	12/4/18		1.O.R. accidentally injured and evacuated to C.C.S.	A.9. 19.
			Work as yesterday; also digging trench across Railway Embankment and erecting camouflage.	
	13/4/18		Instructions received from C.R.E. for work in Left Sector, Reserve Line, to be handed over to 503 Field Coy. & for 511 Field Co. to take over from 503 Field Co. work in 175th Brigade Area (Front Line).	A.9. 19.
			Work continued as yesterday.	
			L/Cpl. BRADBERRY awarded Military Medal, vide III Corps Routine Order No. 204 dated 12/4/18.	
	14/4/18		3 O.R. wounded by shell fire and 4 animals killed & 1 wounded by shell-fire at Transport Lines.	A.9. 1. 9.
			Falling trees for abatis; wiring Villers Bretonneux defences & erecting R.A.P.; other work as yesterday.	
			Nos. 2 & 3 sections moved to billets at Villers Bretonneux.	
	15/4/18		Tracing sites & trenches in front of Villers Bretonneux under instructions of Battalion C.O.s in Line; erecting R.A.P. & Company Headquarters and constructing splinter-proof walls; digging shell-slits at Divisional Headquarters	A.9. 19.
			Fort Manor Chateau.	
	16/4/18		Lieut. LYON and Sapper SIEBERT killed in action on Railway near Villers Bretonneux; 2 O.R. wounded at Villers Bretonneux.	A.9. 1. 8.

WAR DIARY

INTELLIGENCE SUMMARY.

Army Form C. 2118.

3 FIELD COMPANY R.E.

Place	Date	Hour	Summary of Events and Information	Remarks and references to Appendices
Hut 62 D	16/4/18		Work as yesterday.	J.J.S.
	17/4/18		No.3 Section returned to Camp on instructions of O.C. RE. on account of gas shelling of VILLERS BRETONNEUX.	J.J.S.
			Connecting up posts, siting wire + spidlocking trenches + making Company Headquarters, FRONT LINE (Left Brigade).	
			Digging trenches, improving wire and work on Company Headquarters, FRONT LINE (Right Sector); constructing shelters at 174th Infantry Brigade Headquarters.	
	18/4/18		No.2 Section returned to Camp.	J.J.S.
			Work as yesterday. Also felling trees.	
	19/4/18		Completing Company Headquarters, Bombs boxes, Right Battalion, erecting shelters at Company & Brigade Headquarters. Guarters, overhauling bridging equipment.	J.J.S.
			Inspection of Camp Lines by M.O. i/c + Adjutant 58th Divisional Engineers.	
			2. O.R. admitted to hospital suffering from effects of enemy shell gas.	
	20/4/18		Construction of shelters at 174th Infantry Brigade Headquarters.	J.J.S.
			2 Sections worked. Work handed over to 15th Field Co. R.E.	
	21/4/18		1 O.R. proceeded on Course at III Corps Gas School, L'ETOILE; 1 O.R. to course at III Corps Bombing School, BOUCHON.	J.J.S.
			Company paraded for inspection of arms, box respirators and iron rations. 174th Inf. Brigade.	
	22/4/18		Lecture + demonstration given by O.C. cont on tracing of wire and trenches to officers at Headquarters, 174th Infantry Brigade.	J.J.S.

WAR DIARY

INTELLIGENCE SUMMARY.

(Erase heading not required.)

Army Form C. 2118.

511TH FIELD COMPANY, R.E.

Place	Date	Hour	Summary of Events and Information	Remarks and references to Appendices
Map 62.D.	22/4/18		Providing splinter-proof protection for walls of tents and dugouts; Camouflaging roads at M.30.d.	App 18. App 18.
	23/4/18		3 O.R. admitted to hospital suffering from effects of enemy gas.	
			Woke as yesterday.	
	24/4/18		6 Instructions received from 6 R.B., Dismounted Portion of Coy., including 5 Officers + 85 O.R., proceeded to T.M.d.i.9 (Bois-de-GENTELLES) and manned trenches.	App 18.
			O.C. awarded Bar to Military Cross and Late Lieut. LEDY awarded Military Cross, vide Divisional Routine Orders No 1017 dated 23/4/18.	
			2 O.R. wounded in action.	
	25/4/18		Dismounted Portion of Company in trenches (CACHY SWITCH)	App 18. App 18.
	26/4/18	6:30 am	Dismounted Portion of Company returned to camp on relief by 8th MOROCCAN Regiment. Coy. rested.	
Map LENS (11.)	27/4/18	9. am	Company moved by mech route to RIENCOURT.	App 18.
1/100,000	28/4/18	9. am	Company moved by march route to COULONVILLERS	App 18.
	29/4/18		Company paraded for inspection of arms and box respirators	App 18.
	30/4/18		Squad Drill + training.	

J.J. Symonds
Major R.E.
O/C 511 Field Co.

7

CONFIDENTIAL WO 17

WAR DIARY
OF
511TH FIELD COY. R.E.

FROM 1-5-18 TO 31-5-18

VOL. 16

Army Form C. 2118.

WAR DIARY of INTELLIGENCE SUMMARY.

(Erase heading not required.)

VOLUME 16

Instructions regarding War Diaries and Intelligence Summaries are contained in F.S. Regs., Part II. and the Staff Manual respectively. Title pages will be prepared in manuscript.

Place	Date	Hour	Summary of Events and Information	Remarks and references to Appendices
COULONVILLERS Mob. Lds. 51P.	1/5/18		Company and Rifle Drill; Conference with C.R.E. & Officers of Divisional Engineers on Design & fitting of Trenches.	WTH
	2/5/18		Company and Rifle Drill; Conference with C.R.E. & Officers of Divisional Engineers on "Transport".	WTH
	3/5/18		Company and Rifle Drill; Conference with C.R.E. & Officers of Divisional Engineers on "Dumps".	WTH
	4/5/18		Company and Rifle Drill; Musketry.	WTH
	5/5/18		Church Parade.	WTH
			Mounted Section and Transport proceeded by road to DOURDON Ave.	
Mob-Ariens ad. 51P.	6/5/18		Dismounted portion of Coy. marched from COULONVILLERS to ST RIQUIER, and proceeded by bus to MOUFLERS-AU-BOIS. Thence by march route to billets at MIRVAUX. (T.25, sheet 57P.)	WTH
	7/5/18		No. 2 Section employed on road repairs at MOUFLERS-AU-BOIS; remainder of Coy. improving billets. On instructions of C.R.E., Dismounted Section of Coy. moved to billets at PIERREGOT (T.25.c.)	WTH
	8/5/18		Road repairs as yesterday; improvement of billets. Mounted Section and Transport moved from MIRVAUX to PIERREGOT.	WTH
	9/5/18		Road Repairs by No.1 Section as for No.2 Section yesterday; remainder of Coy. Musketry instruction. 4 animals evacuated to Mobile Veterinary Section.	WTH
	10/5/18		Repair of road as yesterday; fitting up huts at BASSEUX. Squad Drill and Bayonet fighting; R.E. Training; improvement of billets.	WTH

Army Form C. 2118.

WAR DIARY
INTELLIGENCE SUMMARY
(Erase heading not required.)

Place	Date	Hour	Summary of Events and Information	Remarks and references to Appendices
Maj 5F	11/5/18		Road repair as yesterday (3 sections); fixing huts at BENCOURT; overhaul of vehicles	WSHL
	12/5/18		Church Parade; fixing huts as yesterday. 6 animals evacuated to Mobile Veterinary Section	WSHL
	13/5/18		Repair of roads; clearing underground galleries at Mailly-M.-Bois; digging shell slits and making splinter-proof protection against bombs for billets. Warning Order for move of Company received.	WSHL
	14/5/18		8 O.R. arrived as reinforcements from R.E. Base Depot. Works as yesterday. O.C. inspected works in line, HENENCOURT. Orders received to be taken over from 517th Field Co. R.E. Orders received from C.R.E. for Company to relieve 517th Field Coy. R.E. on night of 15th/16th May.	WSHL
Maj 62 P.N.M.	15/5/18		Coy. moved by march route from PIERREGOT to BRISIEUX, sections 3 & 4 proceeding to billets in cellars at HENENCOURT, and remainder of Coy. to billets in Bois-de-HAUT (C.5.6.7.8.) near BRISIEUX. 7 O.R. arrived as reinforcements from R.E. Base Depot. 3 O.R. admitted hospital (P.U.O.); 1 O.R. arrived in hand from 517th Field Coy. R.E.; 2 sections driving deep dugouts at V.30.d.2.6. Coy. took over work in hand from 517th Field Coy. R.E. at V.30.d.2.8.	WSHL
	16/5/18		5 O.R. admitted hospital (P.U.O.) Works — Reconstruction of deep dugouts as yesterday; wiring and taping new trenches; erecting medium bridge	WSHL

WAR DIARY
INTELLIGENCE SUMMARY

Army Form C. 2118.

Instructions regarding War Diaries and Intelligence Summaries are contained in F. S. Regs. Part II. and the Staff Manual respectively. Title pages will be prepared in manuscript.

(Erase heading not required.)

Place	Date	Hour	Summary of Events and Information	Remarks and references to Appendices
Map 62.D. N.W.	16/5/18		O/C MURRAY TRENCH and AUSTRALIA STREET; cutting firesteps and lowering parapet, MELBOURNE TRENCH; standing by for demolition parties in HENENCOURT and MILLENCOURT	A/T/L
	17/5/18		8. O.R. admitted hospital (sick); casualty - 1. O.R. wounded in action. Constructing deep dugout at V.30.6.2.6; construction of shelters for R.A.P.; erecting bridges as yesterday; improving and wiring MELBOURNE TRENCH; making chevaux-de-frise.	1/T/L
	18/5/18.		1. O.R. admitted hospital (sick). Wiring and improving MELBOURNE Trench; constructing R.A.P.; making chevaux-de-frise; picketing Overland Track and bridging trenches; wiring in front of CAREY TRENCH.	1/T/L
	19/5/18		6. O.R. admitted to Hospital (sick). Wiring and improvement of MELBOURNE trench; erection of R.A.P., as yesterday. Digging new Outpost line.	1/T/L
	20/5/18		6 animals evacuated to Mobile Veterinary Section. Wiring + improvement of MELBOURNE TRENCH + constructing R.A.P. as yesterday; improving and gas-proofing R.E. dildo in HENENCOURT; making chevaux-de-frise. 8 Remounts received.	15/T/L
	21/5/18.		Dumps made of gas in urns and of wiring material lying in forward area. Wiring, digging and improving trenches; wiring CAREY STREET and SWAN TRENCH; excavating for shelters (MELBOURNE)	15/T/L

WAR DIARY
INTELLIGENCE SUMMARY.

Army Form C. 2118.

Instructions regarding War Diaries and Intelligence Summaries are contained in F. S. Regs., Part II. and the Staff Manual respectively. Title pages will be prepared in manuscript.

Place	Date	Hour	Summary of Events and Information	Remarks and references to Appendices
Map ½ 2ᵈ N.W.	21/5/18 (Cont)		TRENCH); cutting gaps in wire and preparing L.G. positions.	
	22/5/18		H.O.R. admitted to Hospital (sick).	
			Improving trenches; connecting up front line trench; wiring; clearing field of fire by cutting standing crop; erecting shelters.	15THL
	23/5/18		Improving and erecting wire; improving trenches and Outposts Line; clearing field of fire + erecting shelters.	15THL
	24/5/18		Nos. 1 & 2 Sections relieved Nos. 3 & 4 Sections in Works; formed 2 Sections proceeding to billets in HENENCOURT and latter 2 to BOIS-en-HAUT.	
			Deepening and widening trenches; making barbed wire concertinas; providing accommodation for garrison of MELBOURNE TRENCH; sandbagging + fitting door to shelters at Battalion Headquarters, W.25.a.9.5. Instructions received from C.R.E. for relief to be carried out between 511ᵗʰ Field Coy and 503ʳᵈ Field Coy. on 28ᵗʰ/29ᵗʰ May.	15THL
	25/5/18		Deepening, widening and improving trenches; wiring and making concertinas, sandbagging shelters; constructing splinter-proof shelter in MELBOURNE TRENCH for Signal Office.	15THL
	26/5/18		Deepening, widening and improving trenches; wiring; excavating for and constructing box drains; making shelter-frames + concertinas; excavating for large English shelter for higher Battalion Headquarters.	15THL
	27/5/18		Deepening and improving MELBOURNE Trench; starting of hinbays; shuttering roof of concrete M.G. emplacement;	15THL

WAR DIARY or INTELLIGENCE SUMMARY

Army Form C. 2118.

511TH FIELD COMPANY, R.E.

Place	Date	Hour	Summary of Events and Information	Remarks and references to Appendices
Maps 62 D & 57 P	27/3/18 (Cont)		Conducting box drains; making shelter frames and ventilators.	WSHL
	28/3/18		No. 3 & 4 Sections moved from Camp in Bois-le-Haut to Allietto in Warloy. Work on fence, Right Brigade sector; handed over to 503 Field Co. RE.	
			Secs 1 & 2 Sections moved from Allietto at Henencourt to Warloy. Work for Company in Divisional Reserve taken over from 504 Field Co. RE	WSHL
	29/3/18		Lieut. HUGHES, R.E., admitted to hospital, sick. Excavating for and erecting shelters for Divisional Headquarters; deepening SYDNEY STREET C.T.	WSHL
	30/3/18		O.C. left Unit to proceed on leave to U.K. (leave granted 1/2/18 to 15/4/18.) Instructions received for Co. R.E. for work in Line (Right Brigade sector) to be handed over to 80th Field Co. RE on 1/4/18 and for some of Coy. from Warloy to Camp near Bois Robert	WSHL
	31/3/18		Work as yesterday, with addition of fire-stepping MURRAY TRENCH from Y.24.6.8.3 to W.19.a.3.5. Capt. LACE went round work in line with O.C. 80 Field Co. R.E., handing over thankment formwell. Excavation & erection of shelters for Divisional Headquarters.	WSHL

W.N.Lace
Captain, R.E.(T)
acting O.C. 511 Field

Vol 76

WAR DIARY
OF
511TH (LONDON) FIELD COY R.E.
FOR PERIOD 1-6-18 TO 30-6-18

Vol. XVII

Army Form C. 2118.

WAR DIARY
INTELLIGENCE SUMMARY.
(Erase heading not required.)

Instructions regarding War Diaries and Intelligence Summaries are contained in F. S. Regs., Part II. and the Staff Manual respectively. Title pages will be prepared in manuscript.

VOLUME 17.

Place	Date	Hour	Summary of Events and Information	Remarks and references to Appendices
FRANCE.				
MAP. 62 D.	1/6/18.		Work in BAIZIEUX SYSTEM (Reserve Trenches) handed over to 80th Field Co. R.E.	
			Work in BAIZIEUX SECTOR, WARLOY AREA, taken over from 92nd Field Co. R.E. — O.C. went round work.	
			Reconnoitring, surveying and covering large English shelter at Divisional Headquarters, U.21.d.2.9.	
			Dismounted portion of Coy. moved from billets in WARLOY to camp in Sunken Road, at C.10.a.5.0.	
	2/6/18.		Preparing site for canvas camp at C.14.c.7.2.; constructing bomb-proof shelters at Coy. Horse Lines;	
			excavating and timbering shaft at BAIZIEUX MILL O.P. (D.1.a.6.7.) & connecting entrance to chamber.	
	3/6/18.		12. O.R. attached to 114th Infantry Brigade for instructional purposes.	
			Dismantling, removing and preparing new sites for NISSEN Huts; excavating & lining centre shafts and	
			making loophole at BAIZIEUX MILL O.P.; improvement of Camp & Horse Lines; instructing Infantry.	
	4/6/18.		Work on NISSEN Huts & BAIZIEUX MILL O.P. and instructing Infantry continued as yesterday; preparing	
			site for canvas camp. 2 Sections on R.E. Training.	
Sheet 57 D.	5/6/18.		Coy., including Mounted Section, moved to camp in DAILY MAIL WOODS, T.20.a.3.0.	
			12 O.R. rejoined Coy. from Battalions of 114th Infantry Brigade.	
	6/6/18.		Squad, Coy. and Rifle Drill; improvement of camp.	
	7/6/18.		Bridging equipment returned to Coy. from Army Headquarters. Squad, Coy. & Physical Drill; R.E.	
			Training; Lecture on control of rifle fire. O.C. attended conference with C.R.E.	

Army Form C. 2118.

WAR DIARY
INTELLIGENCE SUMMARY
(Erase heading not required.)

Place	Date	Hour	Summary of Events and Information	Remarks and references to Appendices
Shut 57.D	8/9/18		Training as yesterday, except for lecture.	
			O.C. proceeded with Divisional Officers to reconnoitre 31st French Corps Area.	
			Rehearsal of Inspection Parade by Corps Commander to be held on 9/9/18.	
			21 O.R. arrived as reinforcements.	
	9/9/18		Church Parade; Inspection and presentation of medal ribbons by Corps Commander at T.28.b.5.5.	
			Lieut. BEVIS proceeded on reconnaissance of 31st French Corps Area.	
			Lieut. HUGHES rejoined Unit from No.141 C.C.L.	
Nr. AMIENS	10/9/18		Company moved from DAILY MAIL WOODS to ST PIERRE-À-GOUY (B.1) - Dismounted portion by march route and bus to PICQUIGNY, and transport by march route.	
	11/9/18		Reconnaissance and repair of water supply in ST PIERRE-À-GOUY, FOUDRINOY, CAVILLON, BREILLY and CROIX. Pontooning and trestle-bridging.	
	12/9/18		Repair of water supply continued. Pontooning and trestle-bridging; demolitions and wiring.	
			Training of O.R.s inspected by Chief Engineer and C.R.E.	
	13/9/18		Training as yesterday.	
	14/9/18		Tactical exercise carried out in FLUXICOURT - CAVILLON - ST PIERRE-À-GOUY Area.	
	15/9/18		Tactical exercise continued as yesterday; Corps Commander present.	

Army Form C. 2118.

WAR DIARY
INTELLIGENCE SUMMARY.
(Erase heading not required.)

Instructions regarding War Diaries and Intelligence Summaries are contained in F. S. Regs., Part II. and the Staff Manual respectively. Title pages will be prepared in manuscript.

Place	Date	Hour	Summary of Events and Information	Remarks and references to Appendices
Hqs. AMIENS.	15/6/18		Warning Order received from C.R.E. for move of Coy to MOLLIENS-AU-BOIS Area.	
	16/6/18		4 L.D. horses received as Remounts. Mounted portion of Coy proceeded by march route to BAIZIEUX Area, staying at MOLLIENS-AU-BOIS. Nousheing.	
			O.R.S. held Conference with Officers on Tactical Schemes carried out on 2 previous days. O.C. rejoined Unit from on leave to U.K.	
Hqs 62 D	17/6/18.		Dismounted portion of Coy moved from St PIERRE-À-GOUY to BOIS ROBERT (C.11.e.9.3) near BAIZIEUX by march route and 'bus from PICQUIGNY to CONTAY; Mounted section rejoined Coy at BOIS ROBERT.	
	18/6/18		Work in Right Brigade Sector of 47th Divisional Area taken over from 517th Field Co R.E.; reconnaissance of work made by O.S.C. sections and N.C.Os.	
			Nos. 1 & 2 Sections and details of Nos. 3 & 4 Sections proceeded to forward billets in D.19.a.5.1.	
	19/6/18		Excavating for dug-out Chamber Right Battalion Headquarters; excavating & extending sap; excavating shelters, digging drainage and drainage pits at Brigade Baths; patrolling mines on ALBERT-QUERRIEU Road, and extra hauling leads and tamping; Camp improvements. Notification received of award of MERITORIOUS SERVICE MEDAL to Sergt. COOP, J.	
	20/6/18		Shifting, excavating for shelters, improving DOLLY TRENCH; excavating for and erecting shelters; wiring;	

D. D. & I., London, B.C. (A7883) Wt W869/M1672 359,000 4/17 Sch. 52a Forms/C/2118/14

Army Form C. 2118.

WAR DIARY
INTELLIGENCE SUMMARY.
(Erase heading not required.)

Instructions regarding War Diaries and Intelligence Summaries are contained in F. S. Regs., Part II. and the Staff Manual respectively. Title pages will be prepared in manuscript.

511th FIELD COMPANY R.E.

(4)

Place	Date	Hour	Summary of Events and Information	Remarks and references to Appendices
Nob 62.D.	20/6/18 (cont.)		sawing timber and constructing frames for trench shelters; improving dugouts at Right Battalion Headquarters; digging soakage pits and drains at Brigade Baths; patrol and examination of barrage of road mines.	
			16 O.R. arrived as reinforcements.	
			Lieut. D.A. LEWIS transferred to 503 Field Coy R.E.	
	21/6/18		During Russian Sap; improving and fixing shelters in DOLLY TRENCH; patrolling road mines; wiring; improving dugouts at Brigade Headquarters as yesterday; deepening & widening DOLLY SUPPORT & excavating for Loop Headquarters; constructing basket wire concertinas.	
	22/6/18		Notification received of award of MERITORIOUS SERVICE MEDAL to Sergt. WELLS, F.	
			Work on Russian Sap, DOLLY SUPPORT, wiring, construction of concertinas and Brigade Headquarters as yesterday; excavating for shelters in rear of DOLLY SUPPORT; making good damage in "B" Sap.	
			Recent draft instructed in wiring.	
			Vicinity of Camp shelled — one knee wounded and evacuated.	
			Lieut. HUGHES proceeded on leave at II Corps Gas School, L'ETOILE.	
	23/6/18		During Russian Sap, during discussion . . "B" Sap fixing shelters in & improving DOLLY SUPPORT, and improving Brigade Hd August — ill as yesterday; construction of dugout at Battalion Headquarters (D.24.a.2.8); work on Loop Trench lines.	
			1. O.R. killed in action near DERNANCOURT.	

WAR DIARY / INTELLIGENCE SUMMARY

Army Form C. 2118.

Place	Date	Hour	Summary of Events and Information	Remarks and references to Appendices
Map 62D	24/4/18		Executing fortifying scheme in DOYLE SUPPORT, during duration in "B" Coy, arrears, improving Brigade field dugout all as yesterday; wiring barbed-wire concertinas; repair of gas blankets. Practise manning of Battle Positions, BRIZIEUX Sector.	
	25/4/18		Notification received of award of DISTINGUISHED CONDUCT MEDAL to Sergt. EVANS, Hs Coy, relieved in line, BRIZIEUX Sector, by 503 Field Coy. R.E.; O.C. instructed work with O.C. 503 Field Coy. R.E. No. 1&2 Sections and composite section Signal Coy at Camp at C.11.c.9.3. Work taken over from 503 Field Coy R.E. Retaining floor & building at baths, BEAUCOURT, deepening & widening trenches, LAVIEVILLE Line; patrolling road mines; constructing cookhouse at Coy. Transport lines.	
	26/4/18		Work in BEAUCOURT Baths. LAVIEVILLE line as yesterday; 4 O.R. of 58th Divisional Reception Camp, MIRVAUX, forwards. Constructing trench Lincoln-houses at Divisional Headquarters; erecting drying room & altering to M. house at Baths & BOIS ROBERT; taping out battle-practice area. L/Cpl. Burr, C., buried at FRANVILLERS COMMUNAL EXTENSION CEMETERY, C.27.d.1.1. Lamp Mallet. 1 O.R. transferred to 503rd Field Coy R.E.	
	27/4/18		Work on Baths at BEAUCOURT & BOIS ROBERT, at Divisional H.Qtrs., on LAVIEVILLE Line & taping out battle-practice area as yesterday; construction of new Bath house at MIRVAUX.	

Army Form C. 2118.

WAR DIARY
INTELLIGENCE SUMMARY
(Erase heading not required.)

Place	Date	Hour	Summary of Events and Information	Remarks and references to Appendices
Map 62.D	28/6/18		Lieut. CANNING left Unit to proceed on leave to U.K.	
			Work at Divisional Hdqtrs., Bois ROBERT & MIRVAUX Botho, and laying new trenches on LAVIEVILLE Line as yesterday; excavating for and erecting NISSEN Huts at Divisional Hdqtrs; improving trenches (VILLA RESERVE & LAVIEVILLE Line).	
			Thunder Section of Coy. moved to Camp at C.5.a.66. & Dismounted Portion to 6.5.6.7.8. (BOIS- LA - HAUT).	
	29/6/18		O.C. & Lieut. HARVEY inspected works on LAVIEVILLE System.	
			C.R.E. & O.C. sited new trench south of SQUARE TRENCH to Divisional Boundary.	
			1. O.R. arrived as reinforcement.	
			Instructions received from 10.R.E. for relief to be carried out with 504 Field Coy. R.E. on 2nd/3rd July.	
			Work as yesterday; also digging new trench in LAVIEVILLE LINE and making entrance to signals cellar in BEAUCOURT	
	30/6/18		1. O.R. received as reinforcement.	
			4. N.C.Os. from 1st Suffolk Pioneers attached for instructional purposes.	
			Work as yesterday; also fixing gas blankets, and cutting crops to improve field of fire in BAIZIEUX System	

T.M.Townley Lt. R.E.
for
Major R.E. (T.)
Commdg. 511 Field Coy. R.E.

Vol 19

War Diary
of
511th (London) Field Co. R.E.
for Period
1-7-18 to 31-7-18.

Vol. XVIII

WAR DIARY

INTELLIGENCE SUMMARY

VOLUME 18

511th FIELD COMPANY R.E.

Place	Date	Hour	Summary of Events and Information	Remarks and references to Appendices
Maps. 62 D & SENLIS.	1/7/18		Lieut. F.P. HUGHES. M.C. rejoined Unit from III Corps Gas School. Court of Inquiry held at Coy. Headquarters on wounding by bombs of 2 horses in charge of 503rd Field Coy.; President - O.C. 511 Field Co. R.E. Works - Inspection and improvement of Baths at MIRVAUX & BOIS ROBERT; erection of mess & kitchens at Reserve Divisional Headquarters; cutting & rolling crops in BAIZIEUX System; fixing gas protection; setting out DARWIN TRENCH; making new Coy. horse lines; Battle Practice with Infantry.	10744
	2/7/18		Work interchanged between 504th & 511th Field Coys. 3 sections proceeded to forward billets at D.10.a. 0.5. Work at Reserve Divl. Headquarters, rolling crops, and making horse lines as yesterday; also improving SHRINE TRENCH.	10744
	3/7/18		Lieut. GARNER, 1/4th SUFFOLK REGT. PIONEERS, attached for instruction. Improving gas protection of Right & Left Battalion Headquarters; wiring PIONEER TRENCH; excavating for shelters; cutting crops; improving forward billets; making new horse lines & erecting splinter-proof walls; improving SHRINE TRENCH; setting out new line of trenches.	10744
	4/7/18		2 Remounts received. Improving forward billets; wiring; improving SHRINE TRENCH; setting out new trench trunk on horse lines as yesterday.	

WAR DIARY
INTELLIGENCE SUMMARY

Army Form C. 2118.

Place	Date	Hour	Summary of Events and Information	Remarks and references to Appendices
Nov. 62 P.7 SENLIS	4/7/18 (Cont)		Providing gas protection for R.A.P.; constructing Signals O.P.; erecting Ritchen in DIRTY TRENCH; cutting through & bridging road at E.7.a.9.8; making buried wire connections.	WJHK
	5/7/18		2. L.D. Horses killed (1 gunshot; 1 accidentally). Work as yesterday, except wiring; also erecting shelters at Brigade Headquarters & in SHRINE & ETHEL TRENCHES; making frames for dugouts.	WJHK
	6/7/18		1. O.R. proceeded to Course at R.E. Training School, ROUEN; 1. O.R. to Course at III Corps Gas School, L'ETOILE. O.C. Mounted Section attended Conference on horsemanship. 1. O.R. arrived as reinforcement. Improving DITTON & SHRINE TRENCHES & erecting shelters; improving bay-forward slit; cutting exits; fitting wings to approaches to trench bridges from Orchard Track; making bomb splinter-proof protection for horse lines. Men of recent drafts received R.E. training.	WJHK
	7/7/18		4. O.R. detached for instruction of Brigade Battle Surplus. 3 Remounts received. Reconnaissance of gaps in wire and requirements in trench notice boards made by O.C. Improving trenches; erection of shelters; fitting wings to trench bridges & instructing of drafts as yesterday. Erecting bunks in T.M.B. Dugout; camouflaging Brigade Headquarters; erection of Bath at D.Q.G.C.; fixing gas curtains.	WJHK
	8/7/18		Practice Training of Battle Station by Company and Brigade Battle Surplus.	WJHK

WAR DIARY
INTELLIGENCE SUMMARY
(Erase heading not required.)

Army Form C. 2118.

511TH FIELD COMPANY, R.E.

Place	Date	Hour	Summary of Events and Information	Remarks and references to Appendices
Maps 62D & SENLIS	9/7/16 (Cont.)		Work on baths & gas protection; and instruction of draft as yesterday.	WTK
	9/7/16		2. O.R. arrived as reinforcements.	WTK
			Improving DITTON & SHRINE TRENCHES & erecting shelters in latter; fixing gas protection to dugouts; making protection trestle at Long Horse Lines; felling trees for demolition on ALBERT ROAD.	WTK
	10/7/16		1. O.R. wounded in action in DITTON TRENCH & evacuated.	
			Improving trenches, erecting shelters, felling trees to form abbitis, & roofproofing as yesterday; excavating both sides at D.G. 6.6.6.; fixing "urups" to gaps in wire; fixing french name-boards.	WTK
	11/7/16		Instructions received from 2d R.E. for relief to be carried out with 503 Field Coy. R.E.	WTK
	12/7/16		Work as yesterday, except felling trees and fixing "urups" to gaps in wire.	
			Relief carried out between 511th & 503rd Field Coys; works reconnoitred by Officers of both Coys.	WTK
	13/7/16		Sections 1, 3 v 4 returned to billets at Bois-la-Haut, C.5.6.7.8.	
			5. O.R. proceeded to course of instruction in use of Lewis Gun at 174th Infantry Brigade L.G. School.	
			Construction of bath-house; provision of gasprotection at M.G. Coy. Headquarters; bunking I.M.B. dug-out; improving DITTON TRENCH & bomb-protection of Coy. Horse Lines.	WTK
	14/7/16		C.R.E. and O.C. reconnoitred works forward and rear.	
			Erecting superstructure for Refilling Point, BEHENCOURT; improving DARWIN TRENCH; erecting kitchens and	WTK

WAR DIARY
INTELLIGENCE SUMMARY

Army Form C. 2118.

Place	Date	Hour	Summary of Events and Information	Remarks and references to Appendices
SENLIS	13/1/18 (Cont)		Camouflaging hut at Advanced Divisional Headquarters; fixing trench boards and wiring up large gaps in wire; improving Coy. Horse lines.	W.T.K.
	14/1/18		O.C. Mounted Section & 1 O.R. proceeded to Course in Horse Management at No. 7 & 8 Veterinary Hospital. No. 1 Section moved to billets at BERTRANCOURT. 1 Officer & 5 O.R., 1/4th SUFFOLK Regt., attached for instruction in replacement of similar ranks returned to Unit.	W.T.K.
	15/1/18		Works as yesterday; also making "disinfecting pit"; improving bomb-protection at Horse lines. Instruction in R.E. work of recent drafts and 1/4 Suffolk Pioneers attached. Demolition Party training with Infantry.	W.T.K.
	16/1/18		Reconnaissance by Section Officers of gaps in wire and trench notice-boards required. Lieut. CANNING rejoined Unit from leave. 1 O.R. rejoined Unit from Gas Course. Work as yesterday; also erection of shelters in & improving LAVIEVILLE TRENCH; improving gaps in wire; BAZIEUX System; instructing Infantry in wiring. 3 O.R. proceeded to Fourth Army Rest Camp; 3 O.R. rejoined Unit from Lewis Gun Course.	W.T.K.
	17/1/18		Work as yesterday. Instructions received for inter-relief between 511th Field Coy. & 564th Field Coy. R.E.	W.T.K.

Army Form C. 2118.

WAR DIARY
INTELLIGENCE SUMMARY
(Erase heading not required.)

Instructions regarding War Diaries and Intelligence Summaries are contained in F. S. Regs., Part II. and the Staff Manual respectively. Title pages will be prepared in manuscript.

Place	Date	Hour	Summary of Events and Information	Remarks and references to Appendices
Hops 62 D4 SENLIS	18/7/18		Relief carried out between 511th and 504th Field Coys. R.E. - 3 Sections proceeded to forward billets at D.19.c.9.8.; No.1 Section moved from BEHENCOURT to Camp at C.5.b.7.8. 4.O.R. proceeded to 17th Infantry Bn. Lewis Gun School for Course; 1 O.R. rejoined Unit from Course at Fourth Army School of Gunnery. Lieut. HUGHES & 1.O.R. attached to Headquarters 58th Divisional Engineers.	WTH
	19/7/18		Work as yesterday; also grading Road Mines. 1 Officer & 4.O.R. American Engineers attached for instructional purposes. Camouflaging ALBERT Road; wiring; driving Russian Saps; improving bomb-protection at horse lines; constructing delousing pit.	WTH WTH
	20/7/18		Work as yesterday; sandbagging & framing shelters; improving forward billets; grading road mines. Lieut. HUGHES rejoined Unit from Headquarters 58th Divisional Engineers; 1 O.R. proceeded to Course at III Corps Gas School.	
	21/7/18		Work as yesterday - except improving forward billets; also repairing trench bridge & fixing trench boards; excavating for shelters.	WTH
	22/7/18		2 Mounted N.C.Os proceeded to R.E. Base Depot, in accordance with A.R.O. 4034. Court of Inquiry held on casualties from Rifle bombing to animals in charge of 504 Field Coy. R.E. - President: O.C. 511 Field Coy. R.E. Work as yesterday; except repairing trench bridge; fixing notice-boards; excavating dug-outs at Sunken A.D.S.	WTH

WAR DIARY
INTELLIGENCE SUMMARY
(Erase heading not required.)

Instructions regarding War Diaries and Intelligence Summaries are contained in F.S. Regs., Part II. and the Staff Manual respectively. Title pages will be prepared in manuscript.

Army Form C. 2118.

511TH FIELD COMPANY R.E.

Place	Date	Hour	Summary of Events and Information	Remarks and references to Appendices
Map 62D SENLIS	23/7/18		1. L.D. Horse received from 503rd Field Coy. R.E. 16. O.R. Demolition Party, attached to 8th Battn. London Regiment. No.1 Section promoted to Forward Billets. No.2 Section returned to Coy. Headquarters. No.5 & No.7.S. Works: Sinking A.D.S.; completing shelters at Right Battn: Headquarters; constructing delousing pit; excavating for Signals O.P.; wiring; driving Russian Sap; erecting shelters and guarding road mines	
	24/7/18		Work as yesterday.	WTK WTK
	25/7/18		Demolition Party of 16. O.R. co-operated with 8th Battn. in raid on enemy positions in HOOK QUARRY, and later rejoined Coy. — Casualties:– 4. O.R. wounded (1 remained at duty). 1 mounted N.C.O. arrived as reinforcement. Work on trunking, Signals O.P., & Russian Saps continued as yesterday; improving & repairing trenches; replacing road camouflage; improving Forward Billets. 15 American Engineers, previously attached, replaced by similar ranks.	WTK
	26/7/18		Major LACE rejoined Unit from Course in Horse Management. 3. O.R. rejoined from Fourth Army Rest Camp. Major F.J. BYWATER, M.C., O.C. Coy, admitted to No.2 C.C.S., sick. Work on Saps, improvement of trenches & Signals O.P. continued as yesterday. Improving gas-protection at Battn. HQ.: erecting shelters; improving bomb-protection of Coy. Horse Lines. 1. L.D. Horse evacuated to M.V.S.	WTK

WAR DIARY
INTELLIGENCE SUMMARY
(Erase heading not required.)

Army Form C. 2118.

Place	Date	Hour	Summary of Events and Information	Remarks and references to Appendices
Map 62 D + SENLIS	27/7/18		Lieut. F.M. HARVEY admitted to 1st H.C.C.S., sick.	
	28/7/18		4 N.C.O. Instructors at 174th Infantry Brigade battle Surplus reported Unit on refitment. Work as yesterday; also providing chevaux-de-frise for gaps in wire.	WTHL
			Lieut. C.M.D. DAVIDSON proceeded to ENGLAND for duty with Inland Transportation Service. No. 4 Section returned to billets at Brig. Headquarters on relief by No. 2 Section.	
	29/7/18		1 Officer + 5 O.R. 11th Suffolk Regt (Pioneers) attached to Bn. in replacement of similar ranks returned to own Unit. Works:- Providing shelters at Signals O.P.; alterations to gas-curtains at Battalion Headquarters; guarding Road Trees (work interrupted by operations on Right of Brigade Sector). 1 Mounted N.C.O. joined Unit as reinforcement; 1 O.R. returned from Course at III Corps Gas School. Placing Russian Saps; improving, firestepping and repairing trenches; improving burst-protection at Bn. transport Lines; repairing trench bridges; other works as yesterday.	WTHL
	30/7/18		Relief carried out between 511th + 503rd Field Coys. R.E. - O.C. reconnoitred work handed over to Bn. No. 2 Section returned to rear billets. Work on Saps, gas-curtains + burst-protection units as yesterday; also making chevaux-de-frise and placing same in Front Line across DERNANCOURT Road.	WTHL
	31/7/18		No. 2 + 4 Sections proceeded to billets + work at BARLINCOURT + BEHENCOURT, respectively. Nos. 1 + 3 Sections returned to Rear Bn. Billets.	WTHL

Army Form C. 2118.

WAR DIARY
INTELLIGENCE SUMMARY
(Erase heading not required.)

(8)

Place	Date	Hour	Summary of Events and Information	Remarks and references to Appendices
Moly 62D.7 SENLIS.	30/1/18 (Cont)		Works - Constructing Refilling Point at BETTENCOURT and sidings at BAVELINCOURT; improving bond protection at hoy. Transport Lines.	WNL

M.F.Kace
Acting O.C. 511 Field Co. R.E.
Captain R.E. (T.)

58th Divl. Engineers.

511th FIELD COMPANY

ROYAL ENGINEERS

AUGUST 1918

Army Form C. 2118.

WAR DIARY
INTELLIGENCE SUMMARY
(Erase heading not required.)

Volume 19

Place	Date	Hour	Summary of Events and Information	Remarks and references to Appendices
Map 62 D	1/8/18		Warning Order received from C.R.E. for relief of Divisional Engineers by 12th Divisional R.E. on 2/3rd August. Advance Party proceeded to new area. Officer & O.R. of 4th Suffolk Regt. (Pioneers) rejoined own Unit.	
			Construction of Refilling Points at BAVELINCOURT and BEHENCOURT; making and placing chevaux-de-frise in BAIZIEUX system; improving tent-protection to transport lines.	J.H.
	2/8/18		Work on Refilling Points completed. 6th day work handed over to 70th Field Coy. R.E.	J.H.
	3/8/18	12.15 am	Coy. moved from Bois-la-Haut to HAVERNAS by march route and bus. Lieut. C.D. JENKINS joined Unit from R.E. Base Depot.	J.H.
Map 62 D N.W.	4/8/18 8.h.		Coy. moved from HAVERNAS to ESCARDONNEUSE WOOD, near LA HOUSSOYE, arriving at 4.30 am on 5/8/18.	J.H.
	5/8/18		5 O.R. proceeded to Fourth Army Rest Camp; 1 O.R. to course at R.E. Training School, ROUEN; 1 O.R. to ENGLAND to qualify for Commission in R.A.F.	J.H.
	6/8/18		Capt. LAGE & Lieut. JENKINS reconnoitred line. Carrying forward material for repair of CORBIE-BRAY Road; erecting hoop. lamps and providing dust-proof walls to Camp & Horse Lines. Lieut. F.P. HUGHES, M.C., & Sapper COBBOLD wounded in action near SAILLY-LE-SEC.	J.H.

WAR DIARY
INTELLIGENCE SUMMARY

Army Form C. 2118.

511th FIELD COMPANY R.E.

Place	Date	Hour	Summary of Events and Information	Remarks and references to Appendices
Map 62.D.N.W.	1/8/18		Lieut. G. Doyle attached from 503rd Field Coy. R.E. for duty	
			Lieut. HUGHES M.C. died of wounds in Casualty Clearing Station.	
			Gasproofing dugouts at J.29 and J.35; improving camp & horse lines; carrying forward material for road repairs.	A.9.18
	8/8/18		Sections standing by - no work done.	A.9.18
	9/8/18		Gas-proofing entrances to Brigade Headquarters; constructing front-protection of horse lines; 2 sections standing by	A.9.18
	10/8/18		As yesterday	A.9.18
	11/8/18		Carrying forward material for wiring front line; digging standard trench at K.17.a.8.8.; preparing camp for 1 section R.E. in ROMA TRENCH.	A.9.18
	12/8/18		Lieut. LACE and party proceeded to billets at GENT COPSE. Lieut. JENKINS & party to ROMA TRENCH. Wiring front line, and strong point at K.17.b.8.8.	A.9.18
	13/8/18		Sections returned from GENT COPSE and ROMA TRENCH to camp in ESCARDONNEUSE WOOD.	A.9.18
	14/8/18		O.C. rejoined Coy. from Fourth Army Convalescent Camp. Jaffers noted.	A.9.18
	15/8/18		Lieut. DOYLE rejoined 503rd Field Coy. R.E. 1.O.R. proceeded to Course at III Corps Infantry School; 1.O.R. carried as reinforcement. Company rested.	A.9.18

WAR DIARY
INTELLIGENCE SUMMARY.
(Erase heading not required.)

Army Form C. 2118.

Instructions regarding War Diaries and Intelligence Summaries are contained in F. S. Regs., Part II. and the Staff Manual respectively. Title pages will be prepared in manuscript.

Place	Date	Hour	Summary of Events and Information	Remarks and references to Appendices
Map 62.D N.W.	16/8/18		Lieut. C.M. HAKE joined Coy from R.E. Base Depot as reinforcement.	F.J.R.
			Company Drill.	
	17/8/18		Company Training. 3. N.C.Os detached for instruction in Bridging of American Engineers.	D.R.
	18/8/18		Church Parade. 5. O.R. rejoined Coy from Lords (Army Rest Camp)	
	19/8/18		Party of 1 N.C.O. & 2 Sappers attached to each of 6th, 7th & 8th Battns London Regt for instructional purposes.	
			Company Training in R.E. work.	
	20/8/18		Company Training in R.E. work.	
	21/8/18		R.E. Training. Filling in Mine Craters at La HOUSSOYE. 2 Remounts received.	F.J.R.
	22/8/18		R.E. Training.	
	23/8/18		As yesterday.	
	24/8/18		Coy. marched from ESCARDONNEUSE WOOD to J.8.b.3.5.; Transport remained at that location & dismounted portion of Coy. proceeded to camp at CEMETERY COPSE (J.24.b.20.25); Nos. 2 & 3 Sections moved to BRICKYARD at K.16.c.8.7.	
			1 animal killed & 3 wounded (one afterwards destroyed) by hostile bomb.	
	25/8/18		Reconnoitring for shelters at Divisional Headquarters; improving Coy. billets & providing bomb-protection; reconnaissance for dug-out accommodation.	

WAR DIARY / INTELLIGENCE SUMMARY

Army Form C. 2118.

Place	Date	Hour	Summary of Events and Information	Remarks and references to Appendices
Map 62.D.N.W.	25/8/18		One Section proceeded to Brigade Headquarters at L.1.c.3.0., and thence to F.28.d.1.2. Headquarters & 1 Section moved to Hutts at BRICKYARD & Horse Lines moved to near CEMETERY COPSE.	J.1.8
	26/8/18		Headquarters & 3 Sections moved to billets at I.8.a.2.8. 4 O.R. arrived as reinforcements. 2 O.R's (wounded) evacuated to Mobile Veterinary Section. Works - Filling in shell holes in road and tracks; improving tracks; making ramp down to sunken road & repairing crossing over railway; providing accommodation and anti-gas protection at Brigade Headquarters; improving Coy. billets.	J.3.18
	27/8/18		1 O.R. accidentally wounded. Reconnaissance of Water Supply in L.10.a.4.2. carried out. Improving accommodation at Brigade Headquarters (F.28.d.1.2.) & the Brigade Headquarters at F.30.c.3.0.; repairing roads and tracks.	J.1.18
	28/8/18		Headquarters & 2 sections moved to Camp at F.21.d.3.6. & Transport to I.8.a.2.8. No 4 Section rejoined Coy.) No 2 Section attached to 303rd Field Coy. for work at Divisional Headquarters. Improving water supply at Hutted Camp L.10.a.3.4.; providing further accommodation at & repairing track in front of New Brigade Headquarters; making accommodation at Coy. Camp. Dump carried out in 174th Brigade Area. Reconnaissance for	J.1.8

WAR DIARY
INTELLIGENCE SUMMARY

511TH FIELD COMPANY R.E.

(5)

Army Form C. 2118.

Place	Date	Hour	Summary of Events and Information	Remarks and references to Appendices
Map 62 N.E.	29/8/18		Improving water supply at Auttell Camp and at L.10.a.8.7. No.1 Section proceeded to Headquarters 174th Infy. Brigade; One Section attached to 503rd Field Coy. R.E.	F.J.B
Map 62.C. N.W.	30/8/18		Moved, including Transport, moved to Camp in Valley near BILLON WOOD, A.25.d.1.0. Roofing sheds over engine & pumps at L.10.a.5.4.; cleaning well; erecting troughs and hand pumps; clearing site for bath house; reconnoitring for bathy troops & repairing road in B.19.b, c, & d. No.1 Section attached to 174th Infantry Brigade, and proceeded on Brigade Advance Guard.	F.J.B
	31/8/18		Improving water supply at L.10.a.5.4 & L.10.a.3.8.; erecting bath; repairing roads and tracks in forward area. B.19, B.20, B.25, B.26, B.27 & B.28. Reconnaissance of Overland tracks to forward area.	F.J.B

F.J.Bryson
Major R.E. (G)
Commdg 511th Field Coy. R.E

14   W/21

WAR DIARY
of
511ᵗʰ (LONDON) FIELD Cᵒʸ R.E.(T.)

FOR PERIOD

1-9-18 TO 30-9-18.

VOL. XIX

WAR DIARY

Army Form C. 2118.

Volume 19

Place	Date	Hour	Summary of Events and Information	Remarks and references to Appendices
Map Sheet 62C N.W.	1/9/18		Work handed over to No. 5 Field Coy. R.A.R.E.	
			Work: Erecting bath house; improving water supply; latrining drains; repairing Overland tracks.	MHE
	2/9/18		Conference at Headqrs. 58th Divisional Engineers R.E.	
			No 1 Section rejoined Coy. from attachment to 174th Infantry Brigade as part of Advance Guard.	
			Dismantling & removing pumping plant; salvage operations; bridging equipment assembled at Brickyard Dump.	MHE
	3/9/18		Squad drill and inspection of box respirators.	
			O.C. reconnoitred for sites of camps for 3 Field Coys. in neighbourhood of Junction Wood.	
			2 Sections making Overland track; 2 Sections collecting salvage.	MHE
	4/9/18		Lieut. Avis proceeded on leave to U.K.; 1 O.R. proceeded to course at III Corps Lewis Gun School, GAMACHES. 2 N.C.O.s reduced to ranks for inefficiency under para. 183(2) Army Act.	
			Coy. moved to Camp near Junction Wood.	MHE
	5/9/18		Work as yesterday; also providing accommodation at new Camp. Work as yesterday.	
			Bridging equipment returned to Divisional R.E. Dump.	MHE
	6/9/18		No. 2 Section attached to 174th Infantry Brigade.	
			Work on Baths near HEM WOOD. Work taken over from 520th Field Co. R.E. - O.C. reconnoitred new work.	
			Coy. moved to Camp on road near BOUCHAVESNES.	MHE

Army Form C. 2118.

WAR DIARY
INTELLIGENCE SUMMARY.

(Erase heading not required.)

(2)

Instructions regarding War Diaries and Intelligence Summaries are contained in F. S. Regs., Part II. and the Staff Manual respectively. Title pages will be prepared in manuscript.

Place	Date	Hour	Summary of Events and Information	Remarks and references to Appendices
Map Sheet 62 C N.W.	4/9/18		OC reconnoitred Forward Area. Capt. H.L. BAZALGETTE attached from 504th Field Coy. R.E.	
			Orders received for move of Coy. to vicinity of CURLU WOOD. No. 2 Section moved with 174th Infantry	
			Brigade to Billets near SOREL WOOD.	
			Clearing and repairing roads & tracks; improving water supply.	MHE
Map 62e. N.E.	8/9/18		Capt. W.H. LACE proceeded to take over command of 439th Field Coy. R.E.	
			Coy. moved to camp near NURLU.	
			Work handed over to No.1 Coy. R.A.R.E.	
			Notification received of award of Military Medal to No.553415. 2nd Cpl. WELLS. H, vide III Corps Routine Orders	
			No. 559 dated 5/9/18.	
			Repairing huts at Divisional Headqtrs.; providing accommodation, erecting shelters, etc., at 174th Infty Brigade HQ.	
			erecting Coy. Camp.	
			OC reconnoitred water supply and roads in and forward of GUYENCOURT and SAULCOURT.	MHE
	9/9/18		No. 554109. 2/Cpl. BASSU. P., awarded Military Medal, vide III Corps Routine Orders No. 504 dated 8/9/18.	
			OC reconnoitred water supply in GUYENCOURT & SAULCOURT, & dugouts, roads & tracks in Forward Area.	
			Clearing roads, searching for booby traps and wells, repairing and splinter-proofing huts at Divisional HQ,	
			improving Coy. Camp.	MHE
	10/9/18		Work as yesterday. OC reconnoitred for traps in Decauville tracks and in Nissen huts.	

WAR DIARY or INTELLIGENCE SUMMARY

Army Form C. 2118.

(3)

Place	Date	Hour	Summary of Events and Information	Remarks and references to Appendices
Map Sheet 62cN.E.	11/9/18		In trenches and repairing roads. O.C. reconnoitred roads to Gouzeaucourt.	MAR
	12/9/18		Repairing roads; dismantling & re-erecting water tanks & troughs; constructing Brigade Headqtrs. at LIERAMONT.	MAR
	13/9/18		O.C. connected with Headqtrs. 56. Divisional Engineers to take over duties of Acting C.R.E.	MAR
			Maintenance & repair of roads & construction of Brigade Headquarters. Erecting picket lines.	MAR
	14/9/18		Lieut. BAZALGETTE sent round works on line with C.R.E.	MAR
	15/9/18		Work as yesterday; also erecting dent splinter proof walls to horse lines.	MAR
			3. O.R. joined unit as reinforcements. Lieut. Harvey returned dury. from hospital.	
			Lieut Harvey wounded (remains at duty). One O.R. wounded.	MAR
	16/9/18		Work as yesterday.	MAR
			Work as yesterday; also improving track. Reconnaissance of tracks forward to EPEHY.	MAR
	17/9/18		1. O.R. R.A.M.C. (T) (attached to Water Duty) transferred to 2/3rd Home Counties Field Ambulance.	
			3. animals wounded by shell-fire at forward section billet - one evacuated. 1. O.R. wounded & evacuated.	
			Work on Brigade Headqtrs.; loop horse lines track; roads as yesterday; fixing refuse boards; erecting storage tank at SAULCOURT; making overland loop track.	MAR
	18/9/18		Constructing shelter at Brigade Headqtrs.; making overland loop track; repairing track from SAULCOURT to PEIZIÈRE.	MAR
	19/9/18		1. Animal (wounded 17/9/18) destroyed. 2. O.R. evacuated to hospital. (One wounded - gas).	
			Lieut. BAZALGETTE reconnoitred roads, wells and bridges. Work as yesterday, except on loop track; also fencing water-point.	MAR

Army Form C. 2118.

WAR DIARY
INTELLIGENCE SUMMARY

(Erase heading not required.)

Instructions regarding War Diaries and Intelligence Summaries are contained in F. S. Regs., Part II. and the Staff Manual respectively. Title pages will be prepared in manuscript.

Place	Date	Hour	Summary of Events and Information	Remarks and references to Appendices
Map Sheet 62°N.E.	20/9/18		No 2 section returned Coy. from attachment to 174th Infantry Brigade. 2. O.R. arrived as reinforcements. Improving bivouacs and erecting splinter-proof protection for horse-lines.	M&E
	21/9/18		Lieut. Avis rejoined Unit from leave to U.K.	M&E
	22/9/18		Work as yesterday; also protecting horse lines at Divisional Headqtrs. and collecting salvage. No. 3 section proceeded to STE EMILIE on attachment to 174th Infantry Brigade.	M&E
	23/9/18		Constructing accommodation for Headqtrs. 174th Infantry Brigade; other work as yesterday. Squad and rifle drill; collecting salvage; preparing accommodation at Divisional Headquarters.	M&E
	24/9/18		One O.R. proceeded to R.E. Base Depot for medical re-classification. Headquarters & 2 sections moved to VILLERS-FAUCON by march route, and thence South No. 3 section by 'bus. One section to Camp near MONTAUBAN, Transport proceeding independently to that Camp by road.	M&E
Map 62° N.W			Employed at Divisional Headquarters on preparing accommodation, rejoined Unit.	M&E
	25/9/18		Coy. moved by march route to billets at MÉAULTE.	M&E
Map. Lens 11.	26/9/18		Coy. marched to HEILLY and proceeded by train to SAVY-BERLETTE; thence by march route to NIAGARA CAMP (CHATEAU-de-la-HAIE), near VILLERS-au-BOIS.	M&E
	27/9/18		Major H.L. BAZALGETTE proceeded on leave to U.K. 2. O.R. transferred to 93rd Field Coy. R.E.	M&E
	28/9/18		Coy. rested.	M&E

WAR DIARY
INTELLIGENCE SUMMARY

(Erase heading not required.)

Army Form C. 2118.

511TH FIELD COMPANY R.E.

Place	Date	Hour	Summary of Events and Information	Remarks and references to Appendices
Map LENS. 11.	12/9/18		Advance Party under Lieut. CANNING proceeded to forward Billets.	
			One O.R. rejoined Unit from Horses at No. 7 and 8 Veterinary Hospital.	WH
	30/9/18		Work taken over from 104th Field Coy. R.E. Coy. moved from CHATEAU de la HAIE, dismounted portion proceeding to Billets at MAROC and mounted portion to FOSSE 2.	WH

Williamson, Lieut. R.E.(T.)
Acting O.C. 511 Field Coy. R.E.

WAR DIARY
6 of
511TH FIELD COY R.E
FOR PERIOD
1-10-18 TO 31-10-18

Army Form C. 2118.

511TH FIELD COMPANY. R.E.

WAR DIARY or INTELLIGENCE SUMMARY.
(Erase heading not required.)

Volume 9 (1)

Instructions regarding War Diaries and Intelligence Summaries are contained in F. S. Regs., Part II. and the Staff Manual respectively. Title pages will be prepared in manuscript.

Place	Date	Hour	Summary of Events and Information	Remarks and references to Appendices
Map Sheet 44 A	1/10/18		Repairing & opening mushroom in trenches. Making filling in R.C.P. east of Alley. Making gas store at Brigade Headquarters.	A.S
	2/10/18		Work as on 1st. Sappers underwater during the day to go to Headquarters to stand by for enfilt work on receipt of report of probable enemy retirement. Reconnaissance made of one line taped out of overland track commencement of Dynamite Road.	A.S
	3/10/18		Repairing above track, making french bridges for artillery and filling in shell holes on La Bassée Road.	A.S
	4/10/18		1 Section attached to 19th Brigade. Repairing overland track, and filling in trenches. Forming Overland track – Dynamite Road – N.1.6.8.0. H.33.c.2.7. and H.33.c.4.3.	A.S
	5/10/18		Work on Overland track as above. Lieut. F.C.B. Wills M.C. joined the company with effect from 2/10/18.	A.S
	6/10/18		Work on Overland track as above.	A.S
	7/10/18		Work on Overland track as above and widening Dynamite Road to Vanini Road.	A.S
	8/10/18		Work on Overland track as above and gas protection via 19th Brigade Area. Took over handed over to 503rd Field Coy on occasion of Brigade relief.	A.S
	9/10/18		Preparing accommodation at new Divisional Headquarters Croix 11. & making baths for 19th Brigade.	A.S

WAR DIARY
INTELLIGENCE SUMMARY

Army Form C. 2118.

511TH FIELD COMPANY. R.E.

Volume 19. (2)

Place	Date	Hour	Summary of Events and Information	Remarks and references to Appendices
Map Sheet 44 A	10/10/18		O.C. erected wires on line with C.R.E. Continuation of works making Roads for Brigade. Repairing accommodation for new D.H.Q. Repairing Wells and Pumps at M.15.c.2.3. Fitting Gas Curtains to A.D.S.	App 18
	11/10/18		Work on as the 10".	App 19
	12/10/18		Foot-Bridge erected over LENS CANAL at HARNES. One Section attached to 174th	App 19
	13/10/18		Infantry Brigade. Clearing Roads and filling in shell holes between 174th Brigade Area.	App 19
	14/10/18		Headquarters & two Sections moved to Billets at MAMS COROVE. Two Sections & Transports moved to Foria q.	App 18
	15/10/18		Two Sections of Headquarters returned to COURRIERES. Foot-bridge erected over HAUTE DEULE CANAL.	App 9
	16/10/18		Making ramps & constructing Pontoon Bridge over HAUTE DEULE CANAL. Two further Footbridges erected over same.	App 19
	17/10/18		Headquarters and 3 Sections moved to OIGNIES. Transports & 1 Section remained at COURRIERES.	App 8
Map Sheet 44	18/10/18		Company moved to OLIZIERS. K.34.a.O.9. Repairing craters & opening Roads - 604	App 9 18

D. D. & L., London, E.C.
(A7883) Wt W807/M1672 350,000 4/17 Sch. 52a Forms/C/2118/14

WAR DIARY
INTELLIGENCE SUMMARY

Army Form C. 2118.

511TH FIELD COMPANY R.E.

Instructions regarding War Diaries and Intelligence Summaries are contained in F. S. Regs., Part II. and the Staff Manual respectively. Title pages will be prepared in manuscript.

Volume 19

(Erase heading not required.)

Place	Date	Hour	Summary of Events and Information	Remarks and references to Appendices
Map Sheet 44				
	19/10/18		Less one Section attached to Advance Guard, 174th Brigade.	
			Company moved with main Body of 174th Brigade in pursuit of enemy with one Section in advance guard. Craters filled in on our route, two Streams bridged and	J.J.S
	20/10/18		two large fires extinguished. Billets for the night at G.3.c.4.8.	
			Work on Roads. Bridge constructed over stream at ROUPION, for M.T. and Guns	J.J.S
	21/10/18		Company less 1 Section moved to RUMEGIES. Work taken on over Company Constructing	
			Bridge decked ped over stream at RUMEGIES I.7.b.2.3 and at ORCHIES H.13.c.0.0.	J.J.S
	22/10/18		Work as yesterday	J.J.S
	23/10/18		Work as yesterday clearing sites, cutting banks & erecting Bridge at H.6.b.2.8.	J.J.S
	24/10/18		Work as yesterday. Also repairing Bridges at G.11.a.3.1. - Constructing Box Drain through	J.J.S
			fallen in crater at G.16.c.6.8. - Yellow Iron Crater at G.16.b.4.7.	
	25/10/18		Scribbling-crete of Bridge at H.12.c.0.0, completing Bridge at H.6.b.2.8. Reinforcing	J.J.S
			and forming Pontoon Park at RUMEGIES	
	26/10/18		Removing swivels, clearing streams and making up roadways of new Bridge at	
			H.6.b.2.8. Making up Road at new Bridge at I.7.a.3.2. Loading up Heavy	J.J.S
			Bridging Timber at TEMPLEUVE DUMP. Scribbling Bridge at H.13.c.0.0.	

WAR DIARY
INTELLIGENCE SUMMARY.
(Erase heading not required.)

Army Form C. 2118.

511TH FIELD COMPANY. R.E.

Volume 19 (4)

Place	Date	Hour	Summary of Events and Information	Remarks and references to Appendices
Map sheet 44	27/10/18		Reconnoitring Road forward towards MAULDE. Loading Heavy Bridging materials.	A.919
	28/10/18		Dismantling O.B. Section Eucken. One Section moved to forward Billets at GUESNEY I.6.c.1.3.	A.918
			Work as yesterday, stabbing Craters with limestone at 17.6.2.6. Repairing Road approaching at B.2.7.6.6.7. Erasing markings of Bridge at G.11.a.3.2.	A.918
	29/10/18		Constructing Raft Ferry from flying pontoons RIVER SCARPE at J.10.c.5.0. Valance computing a making sections of DECOURS CANAL for Bridge at J.c.3.4.0. Two Sections standing by for Bridging. 1 Section training.	A.918
	30/10/18		Establishing Pontoon Ferries over RIVER SCARPE at J.10.c.5.0. Repairs to floating Bridge over DECOURS CANAL at J.c.3.4.0.	A.919
	31/10/18		Repairing trestles for footbridge over RIVER SCARPE at J.10.c.5.0, and erecting same. Moving Pontoon Ferry over DECOURS CANAL at J.10.c. - Preparing barrels for Barrel Rafts to cross the SCHELDT.	A.919

J.J. Rivers
Major R.E. (T)
O/C 511th Field Co. R.E.

WAR DIARY

of

511th Field Company R.E.

for the period

1.11.18 to 30.11.18.

WAR DIARY
INTELLIGENCE SUMMARY
(Erase heading not required.)

Army Form C. 2118.

511th Field Co. R.E.

Place	Date	Hour	Summary of Events and Information	Remarks and references to Appendices
Map Ref Sheet 44.	1/11/18		Constructing float rafts for use on River SCARPE. Repairing trestles for Trevium Bridge over SCARPE at J.10.c. and repairing floats on River.	MCE
	2/11/18		Tracking Divis. Engr Trestles at H.B. & St. Pair London Road at I.9.c. Constructing and experimenting with Barrel Rafts on Scarpe. Repairing footbridge over SCARPE at J.10.c.5.0.	MCE
	3/11/18		Constructing Rafts & work on Trestles for Trevium Bridge.	MCE
	4/11/18		Constructing Rafts & making Anti-Gas Trestles on Road HB.	MCE
	5/11/18		Work as yesterday.	MCE
	6/11/18		Work as yesterday. Also demonstrating use of Rafts to 6th, 7th & 10th Battalions.	MCE
	7/11/18		Building Barrows Trestle Rafts and demonstrating use of same to Infantry. Further work. Further Construction of & demonstrating with rafts. Forming floating Bridges at RONGY CHATEAU – 1 Section moved to forward billets at MAULDE.	MCE
	8/11/18		Remainder of Company moved to MAULDE. Trucking Bridges for Sykes's concentric footbridge at J.10.c. to take Bob Lank traffic. Establishing Raft Ferries at J.9.b & 8. Constructing Cannon Footbridge at RONGY CHATEAU. Constructing trestles for Bridge over RIVER SCHELDT at MORTAGNE. Establishing Ferry Rafts & making 8" Team infantry over SCHELDT. Constructing footbridge over SCHELDT.	MCE

WAR DIARY
INTELLIGENCE SUMMARY.
(Erase heading not required.)

Army Form C. 2118.

311th Field Co. R.E.

Place	Date	Hour	Summary of Events and Information	Remarks and references to Appendices
Sheet 44.	9/11/18		Company moved to PONT-DE-CANNELLE at O.15.a.9.8. Took on horses from MAUDE	MHE
			to CALENNELLE. Constructing heavy Bridge over ANTOING CANAL at CALLENELLS	
Sheet 38	10/11/18		Company less 1 Section moved to BELOEIL. ECACHARIES at B.14.b.6.2. Removing	MHE
			bottom completing Bridge at CALENNELLE and supporting approaches to same	
			Bridge completed over BLATON-ATH CANAL at B.14.b.6.	MHE
	11/11/18		Company, less 1 Section moved to RUE-BASSE at B.16.b.6.59. Removing	MHE
			from unoccupied road mines and making roadways round mine craters.	
			Remaining Sections rejoined Company	MHE
	12/11/18		Reconnoisance Parties a Section Company drill	MHE
	13/11/18		Constructing Bridge over Brader at Expo Basse B.4.b.85.10	MHE
	14/11/18		Further work on Bridge over Drain & clearing roads already done to allow bridge to	MHE
			carry heavy loads. - O.C. proceeded on 14 days Leave to U.K.	
	15/11/18		Work as yesterday.	MHE
	16/11/18		Work as yesterday. Killing in 4 mine craters and repairing culvert at B.11.a.4.4.40	MHE
			also 17 ton load.	

Army Form C. 2118.

WAR DIARY
INTELLIGENCE SUMMARY.
511th Field Co. R.E.

(Erase heading not required.)

Place	Date	Hour	Summary of Events and Information	Remarks and references to Appendices
Sheet 3F.	17/11/18		Building 10 Ton Bridge over stream at B.10.b.7.8. Young Lieutenants & repairing	MHR
	18/11/18		approaches to Brokover bridge. Building 5 Ton Bridge over stream at B.N.o.17. Completing stone 5 ton Bridge. Reconnecting bridge on C.P.a.6.2 to take 14 tons. Chairing site of old bridge over stream at B.10.b.7.8. & erecting new bridge to take 12 tons	MHR
	19/11/18		Further work on 12 ton Bridge and reconstructing Bridge at C.3.6.6. to carry 10 ton load	MHR
	20/11/18		Work as yesterday	MHR
	21/11/18		Forming approaches to Bridge at B.10.b.7.8 & work on 10 Ton Bridge on C.3.b.6.6.	MHR
	22/11/18		Work as yesterday	MHR
	23/11/18 to 28/11/18		Military & Physical training Sports &	MHR
Sheet H.H.	29/11/18		Company moved to WIERS at H.4.b.4.8.	MHR
	30/11/18		Military & Physical training Sports &	MHR

W.A. Cowan
Capt. R.E.(T)
A/o.b. 511 "Field Co" R.E.

WAR DIARY

INTELLIGENCE SUMMARY.

511TH FIELD Co R.E.

(Erase heading not required.)

Army Form C. 2118.

511TH FIELD COMPANY, R.E.

Place	Date	Hour	Summary of Events and Information	Remarks and references to Appendices
SHEET 44. K.4.b.4.8. WIERS	1/12/18		Church Parade. Party of 1 Officer & 50 O.R. of 144th Infantry Brigade Engrs. reported for instruction in Engineering Trades.	WHE
	2/12/18		C.E. appointed Acting C.R.E. 50th Division	WHE
	3/12/18		Attending & referee to theatre at WIERS	WHE
	4/12/18		Work on construction of Baths on BERDEIL (Sheet 28. B.14.b). Clearing debris of demolished Bridge at J.9.d.5.9. - Clearing site & reconstructing trestles for 10 ton Bridge at E.29.a.6.0. (Sheet 44)	WHE
	5/12/18		Section 1 returned to WIERS from MORTAGNE. Work on Baths at BERDEIL. Giving Lectures for Infantry Battalions at PERUWELZ. (Sheet 44. Ref. L.3.a) Further work Reconstructing Bridge to carry 10 ton Cole Loads at E.29.a.8.0. Further work on Baths at BERDEIL & latrines at PERUWELZ	WHE
	6/12/18		Lieut F.C.B. WILLS M.C R.E. proceeded on leave to U.K. Lieut Q.S. AXIS, R.E(1) awarded Military Cross. Work as yesterday.	WHE
	8/12/18		Church Parade at WIERS.	WHE
	9/12/18		Party of men returned from BERDEIL having completed work on Baths. Further construction of Bridge at E.29.a.8.0.	WHE

WAR DIARY
INTELLIGENCE SUMMARY — 511TH FIELD Co. R.E.
(Erase heading not required.)

Army Form C. 2118.

511TH FIELD COMPANY. R.E.

Place	Date	Hour	Summary of Events and Information	Remarks and references to Appendices
SHEET AL K.4.b.4.8. WIERS	10/12/18		No. 3 Section proceeded to MAULDE (J.2.a.) for preparation & erection of Workshop and Machinery for training classes. Further work on Bridge at E.29.a.8.0. and on Latrines at PERUWELZ and WIERS	MHC
	11/12/18		Work as yesterday.	MHC
	12/12/18		Preparing approaches to Bridge at E.29.a.8.0.	MHC
	13/12/18		Work as yesterday. Continuation of work on Latrines at PERUWELZ & WIERS	MHC
	14/12/18		Capt. M.H. CANNING, R.E. proceeded on leave to U.K. Work as yesterday.	MHC
	15/12/18		Church Parade at WIERS.	MHC
	16/12/18		Further preparation of approaches to Bridge at E.29.a.8.0. Work on Latrines at PERUWELZ & WIERS.	MHC
	17/12/18		Work as yesterday. Lieut. C.D. JENKINS, R.E. proceeded on leave to U.K.	MHC
	18/12/18		Work as yesterday.	MHC
	19/12/18		General work in Camp. Repairs to Billets, Cables &c.	MHC
	20/12/18		Alterations & repairs to Theatre at WIERS. Work on Electric Installation	MHC
	21/12/18		Work as yesterday. Training tables & forms for 17th Infantry Brigade.	MHC
	22/12/18		Church Parade at WIERS.	MHC

Army Form C. 2118.

WAR DIARY
INTELLIGENCE SUMMARY
(Erase heading not required.)

511TH FIELD COY R.E.

Place	Date	Hour	Summary of Events and Information	Remarks and references to Appendices
SHEET 44.				
	23/12/18		Work on electrical installation & general work in camp	WWR
	24/12/18		Work as yesterday. Section 3 returned from MAULDE. Attached Party of 17a	WWR
			Infantry Brigade returned to MOESNES	
	25/12/18		Church Parade at WIERS. Company Dinner	WWR
	26/12/18		Work on electrical installation & general work in camp.	WWR
	27/12/18		Lieut. C.M. HARE R.E. proceeded on leave to U.K. Erecting disinfection stove	
			at PERUWELZ. Excavating Roadway & removing shell cases at H.6.6.39	WWR
	28/12/18		Further work on Disinfection Stove at PERUWELZ	WWR
	29/12/18		Took a party to repair Church, parade at WIERS	WWR
	30/12/18		Further work on Disinfection House at PERUWELZ	WWR
	31/12/18		Work as yesterday.	WWR

W.W.Cummins
Capt R.E.(T)
O/C. 511th Field Coy. R.E.

Army Form C. 2118.

WAR DIARY
or
INTELLIGENCE SUMMARY. 511st (London) Field Co R.E.
(Erase heading not required.)

Hour, Date, Place	Summary of Events and Information	Remarks and references to Appendices
WIERS. 1/40,000 SHEET 44. Jan 1919. K.14.b.4.8.	During this month the Company generally has been employed as follows. 1 Section at MAULDE finishing and running enemies and workshops for prisoners. Sclools. remainder of Company on general R.E. work e.g. Construction of Bridges at RENGIES and ROUCOURT, Baths at BERDEIN, Divisional Laundry at PERUWELZ, Eleven Light Installation at WIERS. repairs to various at WIERS. repairs and general improvements to Billets and Mess Rooms, giving improvements to RE Workshops at WIERS, and general work on area around Europe. A. M. Hake Lieut. R.E.(?) Commanding 511st Field Co R.E.	9/8/25

511TH
FIELD COMPANY.
R.E.
No. A.8.2
Date 10/2/19

511th Field Company R.E.

WAR DIARY
INTELLIGENCE SUMMARY
(Erase heading not required.)

Army Form C. 2118.

Hour, Date, Place	Summary of Events and Information	Remarks and references to Appendices
INERS. Belgium { 1st Feb. 1919 22nd Feb. 1919 LEUZE. Belgium { 22nd Feb. 1919 28 Feb. 1919	During the month the Company has been employed on general work, dismantling workshops for training of Infantry; checking and overhauling Tool Carts and Equipment, prior to same being handed in to Store; construction of Divisional Concentration Depot at LEUZE, etc. and preparation of new improvements to Billets at LEUZE.	

C.U. Stoke Capt. R.E.(?)
Comdg 511 Field Co. R.E.

Army Form C. 2118.

511th Field Co R.E.

WAR DIARY
or
INTELLIGENCE SUMMARY.
(Erase heading not required.)

Place	Date	Hour	Summary of Events and Information	Remarks and references to Appendices
LEUZE BELGIUM	1 March 1919 to 31 March 1919		The Unit is now down to CADRE STRENGTH. During the month the company has been employed on general works, reconstructing, measuring & valuing huts etc for sale, improvements to billets, overhauling & checking tools & equipment prior to same being handed into stores.	

C.H. Hake Major R.E.(?)
Commanding 511 Field Co R.E.

1st 4. 1919

Army Form C.2118.

Vol 28

53 pu

WAR DIARY
or
INTELLIGENCE SUMMARY.
(Erase heading not required.)

Place	Date	Hour	Summary of Events and Information	Remarks and references to Appendices
LEUZE BELGIUM	April 1st 1919		Company down to CADRE STRENGTH. During the month the men employed on Barrens to evacuating Tournai in preparation for incoming troops. Reconnoitering positions of supply like mines &c around the district, and general regimental work.	
	April 30 1919			

C.W. Hoste Capt R.E.
Commanding 511 Field Co R.E.

511TH FIELD COMPANY, R.E.
No. WD 4/19.4
Date 30.4.19

WAR DIARY
or
INTELLIGENCE SUMMARY.

Army Form C. 2118.

511 F.Coy

(Erase heading not required.)

Place	Date	Hour	Summary of Events and Information	Remarks and references to Appendices
LEUZE BELGIUM	May 1st 1919 to May 31st 1919		For the past month the Horse Strength of this unit has been employed wholly on general regimental duties.	

C.M. Mike Capt RE
Commanding 511 Field Coy RE

www.ingramcontent.com/pod-product-compliance
Lightning Source LLC
Chambersburg PA
CBHW081410160426
43193CB00013B/2144